**Point Reyes lighthouse**

# Point Reyes

## A Guide to the Trails, Roads, Beaches, Campgrounds, and Lakes of Point Reyes National Seashore

**Dorothy L. Whitnah**
**Foreword by Jon Carroll**

 WILDERNESS PRESS • BERKELEY

FIRST EDITION 1981
SECOND EDITION 1985
Second printing May 1987
Third printing December 1988
Fourth printing January 1991
THIRD EDITION April 1997

Photos by Luther Linkhart except as noted
Front cover photo © 1997 by Larry Ulrich
Back cover photo © 1997 by Luther Linkhart
Book design by Kathy Morey
Cover design by Larry Van Dyke

Library of Congress Card Catalog Number 97-7535
International Standard Book Number 0-89997-173-3

Manufactured in the United States

Published by **Wilderness Press**
**2440 Bancroft Way**
**Berkeley, CA 94704**
**Phone: (800) 443-7227**
**FAX: (510) 548-1355**

Write, call or fax us for a free catalog

**Cover photo:** Yellow tree lupines on Pt. Reyes and Point Reyes Beach

**Library of Congress Cataloging-in-Publication Data**

Whitnah, Dorothy L.
    Point Reyes : a guide to the trails, roads, beaches, campgrounds, and lakes
  of Point Reyes National Seashore / Dorothy L. Whitnah. -- 3rd ed.
        p.        cm.
    Includes bibliographical references and index.
    ISBN 0-89997-173-3
    1. Point Reyes National Seashore (Calif.)--Guidebooks.        I. Title.
F868.P9W47        1997
917.94'62--dc21                                                    97-7535
                                                                      CIP

# Special notes

All telephone numbers in this book have area code 415 unless otherwise indicated.

Some of the trail signs in the National Seashore use the metric system.

1 mile = 1.6 km.
1 km. = 0.6 mile

If you are checking the tide tables in a San Francisco newspaper, bear in mind that high tide at Point Reyes is about an hour earlier than at the Golden Gate.

Abbreviations that appear frequently here:

b&b = bed and breakfast
Caltrans = California Dept. of Transportation
GGNRA = Golden Gate National Recreation Area
GGT = Golden Gate Transit
MALT = Marin Agricultural Land Trust
NPS = National Park Service
PG&E = Pacific Gas and Electric Company
PRNS = Point Reyes National Seashore

During recent years West Marin has undergone a series of storms (described in the section on "Climate") which have occasionally closed access roads to the park. After a serious storm, you can call Caltrans at (800) 427-7623 or (415) 557-3755 to find out if any roads are closed.

In October 1995 a horrendous wildfire (described in the Preface to this book) destroyed much of Inverness Ridge and about 15% of the National Seashore. For several days the park was closed. Gradually most of the roads and trails were reopened, although Sky and Coast camps were closed until April 1996. If a similar disaster should again befall the park, call the Bear Valley Visitor Center (663-1092) before planning a hiking or camping trip.

All the campgrounds called "free" in this book will, as of May 1, 1997, cost $10 per individual or family campsite, $30 for a group campsite.

# Acknowledgements

I am grateful to the following persons, who have provided companionship, hospitality, information, and encouragement:

Julia and Peter Allen
Robert and Serena Bardell
Richard A. Brown
Marge Drath
Ira Eisenberg
David and Ellen Elliott
Haskell and Linda Fain
Allan and Mickie Friedman
David and Terry Griffiths
Gordon and Mary Griffiths
Marion and Stephen Gale Herrick
Cecelia Hurwich
Marge Johntz
Gaye Kelly
Luther Linkhart
Rose and Seymour Miller
Arlen and Clare Philpott
George F. Ritchie
Madeleine S. Rose
Jeffrey Schaffer
Shirley Sheffield and Ron Sol
David Weintraub
Ann and Gregory Whipple

Finally, my thanks to the dedicated and hardworking employees of the National Park Service, particularly:

- Superintendent Don Neubacher, who gamely held the National Seashore together during an unprecedented series of calamities;
- Acting Chief of Interpretation John Dell'Osso, who generously gave his time to help clarify for me the park's facilities and regulations;
- and most especially Seashore Historian Dewey Livingston, who has graciously and patiently shared with me over the years his wide knowledge of the early days of Point Reyes.

None of the above is responsible for any errors that may have crept into the book.

——D. L. W.

# Contents

# Foreword

## by Jon Carroll

I don't believe in magic, but I do believe in Pt. Reyes. I believe that magic occurs on Pt. Reyes. It has happened to me; it has happened to others. Since magic is an imaginary phenomenon, it follows that Pt. Reyes is an imaginary place. What you hold in your hands is a guidebook to a fictional peninsula. If it's not there when you arrive, don't say you weren't warned.

I have fallen in love in the deep fog of a Pt. Reyes summer afternoon; I have watched a cow being born in one of its secret bowers. I have seen my daughters dancing on Limantour Beach as the white deer ran across the ridgeline. I have seen huckleberries in such profusion as to suggest divine intervention. I have watched sunsets that lasted longer than the days that preceded them. I have watched a bagpiper blow away to fog on Mt. Vision. I have seen a butterfly ride a snake.

Maybe it's because Pt. Reyes is itself a transient, an outlaw, a stranger passing through town. It is resolutely heading for Canada while the rest of California is on the move toward the tropics. The movement is slow by human criteria but very brisk indeed by geologic standards—it's almost as though Pt. Reyes is skipping town before a tribunal can be assembled to hear the tales of sorcery.

So think of this book as one of those ancient volumes of arcane lore often found in dusty attics. It is chock full of hints and history and directions to places where **X** marks the spot. There is (of course) actual buried treasure on Pt. Reyes, cursed Spanish gold and gems from Samarkand and Xanadu, and there is also unburied treasure, right in front of your eyes if only you know how to look. The location of neither is revealed in this book, but if you spend enough time out on the Point, with an apple and a water bottle and this volume tucked in your daypack, you just might discover it for yourself.

*Pt. Reyes* is a nearly perfect book, and Dorothy Whitnah is a nearly perfect author, although anyone who could call the graceful cow parsnip "vulgar" has clearly not achieved total enlightenment. Let me emphasize a few points. The Pierce Point trail is a four-star, four-boot, worth-a-detour, make-sure-you-go-all-the-way-to-the-end walk. Too many visitors take the other road and head for the lighthouse instead. It's a very fine lighthouse and all, but Pierce Point is a gift. While walking, look for the elk and the bathtub. I can say no more.

And be sure also to at least once come in from the south end of Pt. Reyes on the Palomarin trail—the way the landscape changes about three miles in is worth every switchback.

It is also permissible to go overland in Pt. Reyes. Particularly in the headlands areas like the gentle hills on either side of the Estero Trail, getting lost is pretty darned hard; you can see great distances from any high spot. Remember that mud is a good thing and that animals with udders are peaceful; follow your instincts and make your own adventure.

Walk softly, though. Sing only when necessary. Sit quietly. Carry a tide table. Remember that each trail is a kind of narrative, a tale told by gravity, wildflowers, rodents, vistas, fire, ghosts, sand, madness, egrets, wind. Keep walking and keep listening. If you're not back before the next full moon, we promise not to send out a search party.

# *Preface*

## Paradise gained

As I wander over the hills and marshlands of the Bay Area and watch them every year become covered with more and more tract houses, shopping malls, and gridlocked highways, the existence of the Point Reyes National Seashore seems ever more miraculous—70,000 acres of forests, wetlands, and beaches only an hour's drive from a major metropolitan area.

It almost didn't happen. In the 1950s nearly everyone assumed that West Marin would inevitably be developed along the lines of Carmel-Monterey or the resorts of Southern California. The West Marin Master Plan of 1961 predicted a population of over 60,000, dedicated mainly to serving a tourist and resort visitation of millions. The plan envisaged four-lane highways over the county leading to subdivisions, motels, shopping malls, yacht harbors, and other accouterments of upper-middle-class 20th century life, along Bolinas Lagoon and Tomales Bay.

Yet as far back as 1935 the Department of the Interior had considered Point Reyes a desirable site for a national park. In the 1950s, as lumbering, oil exploration, and site development became increasingly obvious on the peninsula, the residents of West Marin and other conservationists banded together to try to preserve this "island in time." They had the invaluable support of Senator Clair Engle and Congressman Clem Miller. The subsequent negotiations leading to the formation of the park are described later in this book in the chapter "The Making of a Park." Somehow the conservationists and like-minded politicians managed to make a deal with the local ranchers and to stand off the timber, oil, and real-estate interests. Could that happen today? Not bloody likely! Suffice to say that on September 13, 1962, President John F. Kennedy signed the bill authorizing the Seashore.

The late historian of West Marin, Jack Mason, did not use the terms "miracle" or "window of opportunity" when he wrote the epilogue to *Point Reyes: The Solemn Land* in 1970, but these words come to the reader's mind when Mason points out that Clem Miller was killed in an airplane crash in October 1962; in the fall of 1963 President Kennedy planned to visit Point Reyes, but instead changed his itinerary to include Dallas; and Clair Engle died of cancer in 1964. As Mason noted, "Within 22 months of completion of the Seashore legislation, all three of its leading architects were dead."

As we enjoy our National Seashore we should also give thanks to the other public servants—and in this case that term is certainly warranted—who have devoted their time and energy over the years to establishing and preserving it:

- Peter Behr, former Marin supervisor and California state senator, one of the founding fathers of the park;
- the late Congressman Phillip Burton, godfather of the GGNRA;
- his widow, Sala, who succeeded him in office;
- his brother John, now a California state legislator;
- US Senators for California Barbara Boxer and Dianne Feinstein;
- US Representative Lynn Woolsey of Marin County;

- and Marin County Supervisor Gary Giacomini, who served on the board since 1972 as a staunch defender of the environment and a liaison with the ranching community.

## Trouble in paradise: the fire of October 1995

On the afternoon of October 3, 1995, a wildfire began near the summit of Mt. Vision and swiftly sped through the bishop-pine forest of Inverness Ridge. At its fiercest, on October 4, the fire consumed an acre every five seconds. It was difficult to bring under control, partly because of strong, gusty winds and partly because of almost seven decades of accumulated flammable material on the forest floor.

More than 2,000 firefighters from all over the state arrived at Bear Valley headquarters to battle the fire. Almost half of them were inmates from various correctional institutions. Despite the firefighters' backbreaking labor, 45 houses on Inverness Ridge were consumed. The inhabitants of Inverness town were preparing to evacuate when the wind died down and the fog came in. Credit for sparing the town is also due to National Seashore Superintendent Don Neubacher, as reported by David Rolland in the *Point Reyes Light* of October 12:

> Despite the loss of property, Supervisor Gary Giacomini said at a public meeting Sunday that Seashore Superintendent Don Neubacher deserves credit for limiting the destruction.
>
> "If we had a different superintendent, we would have lost Inverness," Giacomini said, explaining that Neubacher wanted firefighters deployed first to protect homes, not the park.
>
> "We would have split our resources to save the park," the supervisor said. "There were horrible decisions to be made with this monster."

Ultimately the "monster" destroyed 12,354 acres before it was finally contained on October 7. The burned acreage included 15% of the National Seashore. The firefighters originally hoped to stop the blaze at Limantour Road, but were unsuccessful; eventually the ultimate firebreak turned out to be Sky Trail. By great good fortune, nobody—neither homeowners nor firefighters—was killed or seriously injured.

Within a week, four 14- and 15-year old boys confessed to having inadvertently started the blaze by camping out illegally overnight on September 30 and building a campfire. When they left the campsite they did what they thought prudent to extinguish their fire, by dousing it with water and covering it with dirt. What they didn't realize—and probably many people, young or old, wouldn't—was that embers can smolder away under pine duff for days. In this case, sudden, gusty winds reached the smoldering embers and caused them to set fire to the surrounding dry brush and bishop pines.

The Marin district attorney decided not to prosecute the teenagers, because they evidently had tried to snuff out their campfire; they were obviously extremely remorseful; and so many people had habitually camped out on that spot—even though illegally—that it might have been difficult in a court of law to prove that no one else could have started the fire.

While the fire was a tragedy to the 45 homeowners on Inverness Ridge – many of whom saw a lifetime's worth of photos, art, letters, manuscripts, and other irreplaceable treasures go up in flames—it was not a permanent disaster to the National Seashore. In fact, it might be considered not exactly a blessing (it did, after all, cost $7 million to suppress) but at least an unprecedented educational opportunity, or an unexpected laboratory in which to watch nature restore itself.

## Effects of the fire: plants

The plants that benefit most obviously from a fire are the bishop pines. These closed-cone pines require intense heat to release their seeds. By 1995 the pine forest on Inverness Ridge was probably in late middle age because fire-suppression efforts had prevented any major fires there for 68 years. A few months after the fire, a multitude of pinelets were already visible under the burned trees. And the coastal scrub—notably the coyote brush—was clearly resprouting.

The best way to investigate this fascinating accidental laboratory is to check the succession of plants over the months and years to come. The park visitor centers will issue regular bulletins and conduct nature walks into the burn area.

Although many visitors volunteered to help in replanting, the park staff decided to let the ecosystem restore itself—which it is rapidly doing. On the other hand, this seems a golden opportunity to enlist volunteers in getting rid of invasive non-native plants. To find out the schedule for this healthful activity, popularly known as "broom bashing," inquire at the Bear Valley Visitor Center.

## Effects of the fire: animals

The NPS has set up infrared cameras around the Seashore which are automatically triggered by creatures moving in front of them. Thus biologists have begun to estimate the effects of the fire on various faunal populations.

Most birds and large animals were able to escape the fire, although the changes in their habitats may result in changes in population, population movements, or population distributions as the months go by. For example, the exotic deer may fare better than the native black-tailed deer if forage becomes scarce.

Small mammals fared much worse. In particular, two rare species of rodent apparently suffered great population loss: the Point Reyes jumping mouse and the *Aplodontia*, or "mountain beaver" (so-called though it is not a true beaver but the most primitive living rodent in the world).

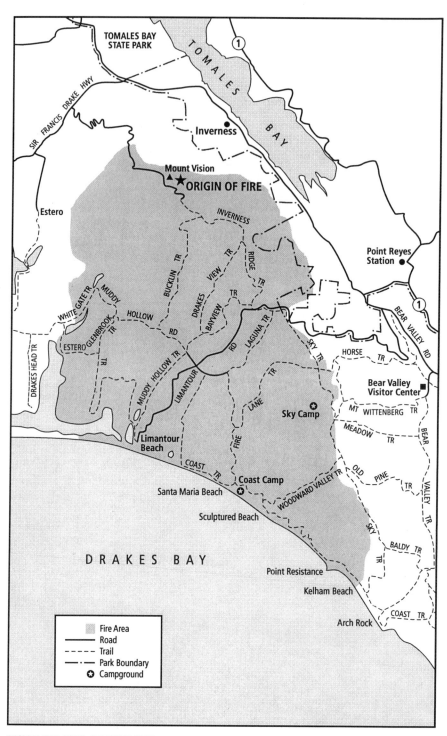

**VISION FIRE AREA, OCTOBER 1995**

# Introduction

## Geology

The Point Reyes peninsula is a place of great fascination for geologists. You can easily see why when you walk (or roll) along the short, wheelchair-accessible Earthquake Trail near the Bear Valley Visitor Center (see p. 43) which runs along the San Andreas fault zone. This landscape dramatically illustrates the concept of **plate tectonics**.

To summarize this concept briefly: The outer layer of the earth, the *lithosphere*, is composed of huge, contiguous crustal plates, about 60 miles thick. These plates are gliding over the *asthenosphere*, a hot, molten layer about 200 miles thick. In some places, two plates meet head on, and one overrides the other, the lower plate diving into the asthenosphere, where it melts (see the figure on p. 2).

In other places, two plates move away from each other. But instead of a fissure developing between them, a ridge develops. This ridge is formed of molten material that comes from beneath the earth's crust and erupts onto the ocean floor (see the figure). In yet other places, two plates glide horizontally past each other. That's what's happening in the San Andreas fault zone, which represents the boundary between the Pacific plate to the west and the North American plate to the east.

The primeval North American continent was originally part of a single supercontinent, which also included primeval Eurasia, Africa, South America, and Antarctica. Roughly 230 million years ago the pieces of this supercontinent began to drift apart, and the North American plate began to override the western, oceanic Farallon plate. For 200 million years the North American plate moved westward, carrying the primeval North American continent atop it. Then, about 30 million years ago, the North American plate overrode the western edge of this east-moving (Farallon) plate and came into contact with the eastern margin of the north-moving Pacific plate. These two plates began to slip laterally past each other. This slippage is still going on, and we call the interface between the two slipping plates the San Andreas fault zone. (Beneath the surface the width of the interface is far greater, and this has led to surface faulting from off the California coast to as far east as western Nevada. This broad fault zone is known as the San Andreas fault **system**.)

At present, the Pacific plate is moving northwest relative to the North American plate at slightly more than 2 inches a year. If this rate had been steady for the entire 30 million years since lateral movement began, total displacement along the fault would have been 1,100 miles, but correlation of similar rock samples on the two sides of the fault suggests a movement of something over 300 miles.

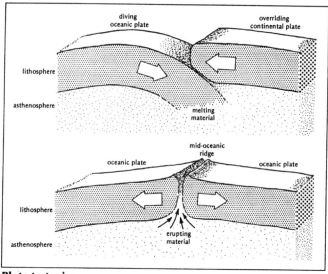

**Plate tectonics**

Although the Pacific plate is generally moving northwest an estimated 2 inches per year, we know that on April 18, 1906, part of it moved as much as twenty feet in just a few moments. This maximum displacement occurred not in San Francisco but in the Olema Valley, just outside what is now the National Seashore.

Certainly the San Andreas fault zone is the most significant—indeed, the determining—feature of the Point Reyes peninsula's general shape. The segment of the fault we are here concerned with runs southwest under Tomales Bay, and continues through the Olema Valley (the route of State Highway 1) and Bolinas Lagoon. The bedrock of the peninsula—granite about 80 million years old—is entirely different from the rock east of the fault, which is rock of the Franciscan Complex (formerly called the Franciscan Formation), a jumble of mainly sedimentary rocks laid down 100–150 million years ago.

The granite was once the core of a high mountain range that lay south of the Sierra Nevada. Through faulting, it was rifted from its original position and transported northwestward—mostly underwater; hence the marine sediments atop it—to its present location. Only for the last 100 or so million years has the right-lateral movement been along the San Andreas fault. In contrast to a mountain origin, the Franciscan Complex had an oceanic origin in a subduction zone (where a diving oceanic plate descends beneath an overriding continental plate—see the figure). It was then later transported northward along a series of faults before the San Andreas fault developed, which juxtaposed the granitic rock northwest alongside a part of it. (Much of the Franciscan Complex has been transferred northward from this area through right-lateral faulting.)

The Loma Prieta earthquake of 1989, which killed 60 people and caused millions of dollars of damage in the Bay Area and the Santa Cruz area, inflicted little damage on the Point Reyes peninsula (other than some cracked roads), because its epicenter was about 90 miles south, whereas the epicenter of the 1906 quake was much closer.

# Topography

The most prominent feature the visitor will notice is densely forested Inverness Ridge, which runs northwest along the peninsula, parallel to the fault zone. Its highest point is Mt. Wittenberg, 1407 feet—a fairly short, scenic climb from park headquarters. On the east, the ridge descends steeply to pastoral Olema Valley; on the west, it descends more gently to rolling pastures and the drowned river valleys and sheltered beaches of Drakes and Limantour esteros.

*Walking beside the rugged cliffs near Sculptured Beach at low tide*

To the northwest, between the ocean and Tomales Bay, lie more pastures and wind-swept moors that have reminded visitors of Yorkshire or Scotland. At the southwestern tip of the peninsula, the rocky promontory of Point Reyes rises 600 feet above the pounding surf. And along the western edge lie miles of white sandy beach—beautiful but wild.

Even casual hikers, bicyclists, and equestrians on the Point Reyes peninsula will notice evidence of the area's unique geology. As you wander along the trails, streams change course abruptly; fresh-water lakes appear in unexpected places; landslides are apparent; and as you picnic on the beach you can watch the cliffs eroding before your eyes (in fact, if you sit too close to them you can actually feel them eroding, as sand and pebbles shower down onto your head and into your drinking cup).

We shall note some of these phenomena as we explore the trails.

### Recommended reading:

Clark, Joseph C., Clyde Wahrhaftig, and Earl E. Brabb, *San Francisco to Point Reyes: Both Sides of the San Andreas Fault.*

California Division of Mines and Geology, 1991. This is an account of a field trip from the division's Special Publication 109: an auto itinerary from San Francisco up Highway 1 to Point Reyes.

Evens, Jules G., *Natural History of the Point Reyes Peninsula*. Rev. ed. Point Reyes: Point Reyes National Seashore Association, 1993. The authoritative guide to the entire natural history of the region; essential reading for anyone who plans to spend much time here.

Galloway, Alan J., *Geology of the Point Reyes Peninsula, Marin County, California*. Sacramento: California Division of Mines and Geology, 1977. Bulletin 202. Paperback. Includes bibliography and elaborate map; usually available at park headquarters.

Wallace, Robert E., editor, *The San Andreas Fault System, California*. Washington, D.C.: US Geological Survey, 1990. Professional Paper 1515. Paperback. This is "an overview of the history, geology, geomorphology, geophysics, and seismology of the most well known plate-tectonic boundary in the world" (quote beneath title). Although it is quite technical, much of it can be readily understood by the interested lay person.

# Climate

Like the rest of the Bay Area, Point Reyes has what is called a Mediterranean climate, characterized by a wet season (roughly October-March) and a dry (roughly April-September). However, the peninsula gets a lot more summer fog than most areas of Mediterranean climate, including some other parts of Marin County. Proponents of Drakes Bay as the great navigator's California landing place put forth as one of their main arguments his annalist's kvetching about the weather: "... notwithstanding it was in the height of Summer, and so near the Sun; yet were we continually visited with...nipping colds...neither could we at any time in the whole fourteen days together, find the air so clear as to be able to take the height of Sun or star..." He complained also about the "thick mists and most stinking fogs."

What this means for the modern visitor is: come prepared for cool weather even in midsummer; bring a sweater or windbreaker, or both. Bear in mind also that the weather frequently varies *within* the park: for example, the beaches may be fogged in while the Olema area enjoys brilliant sunshine. You can phone headquarters (663-1092 or 663-9029) in advance to find out what the weather is like.

The past two decades have witnessed more extreme variations in weather patterns in West Marin than any others experienced since the inhabitants began keeping records.

On January 3-4, 1982, almost 12 inches of steady, pounding rain on the already-soaked ground turned creeks and streams into raging torrents that swept trees, bridges, cars, propane tanks, houses, and everything else before them. Mudslides downed trees and other debris blocked roads, tore down power lines, and disrupted water supplies. The town of Inverness was entirely isolated from the rest of the world for three days, during which a half-dozen houses were totally destroyed and many others severely damaged. Almost miraculously, no one was killed or badly injured, and the stout-hearted inhabitants rose to the emergency by banding together in an inspiring show of community spirit.

In the National Seashore, the main damage was to the Limantour Road and the Bear Valley Trail.

The northern section of the Limantour Road was constructed in 1966, when the park planners were still thoroughly auto-oriented. Even then, environmentalists and downslope property owners objected to the construction of such a broad road on steep and unstable terrain so near the San Andreas Fault. The property owners filed suit to block its construction, but the suit was thrown out because—according to one of them—"the presiding federal judge was incapable of reading a map." During the storm of January 1982 slides occurred on the controversial new part of the road, and the Park Service closed the entire road to the public. Lack of funds prevented repair of the road for over a year, and in March 1983 another slide displaced a further 60-yard-long section of pavement.

Still recovering from the storms of 1982, West Marin in 1983 had to endure

**Hikers on the way to Kehoe Beach**

the wettest winter since anyone started keeping records, plus an unusual combination of winds and high tides. This time Inverness was spared, except for a bit of flooding along Tomales Bay. It was Stinson Beach, to the south of the National Seashore, that bore the brunt of storm damage. Series of huge waves battered the beachfront houses, totally destroying some and rendering others uninhabitable. The residents of the Seadrift development ordered tons of riprap placed around their sandspit, thereby protecting most of their homes. Much of the sand on the GGNRA's part of Stinson Beach was washed out to sea. Drakes Beach in the National Seashore also lost a lot of sand.

February 1986 saw more storms, causing about $4.5 million in damage to public property and roads and about $400,000 damage to the National Seashore. One reason the damage was less than in previous years was that much of the county had instituted extensive flood-control measures after 1982 and 1983. For example, the Park Service protected the Limantour Road by laying huge sheets of plastic—250 feet wide by 100 feet long—over the section that had given way during earlier storms.

Beginning in 1987 Marin, like the rest of Northern California, underwent six years of drought, punctuated by an occasional winter windstorm.

The winter of 1994–95 was even wetter than the ones of the '80s and culminated in another torrential rainstorm accompanied by hurricane-force winds, which wreaked havoc on the area. This storm destroyed several buildings and badly damaged others; downed hundreds of trees; flooded roads; killed dozens of animals, including livestock and seal pups; and cut off electricity to many places, including National Seashore headquarters, for three days.

In October 1995 the Vision Fire, described in the Preface to this book, burned about 15% of the park and forced the closure of many trails and two camps. Before Seashore personnel could begin to cope with the fire damage, the federal government shut down *all* the national parks temporarily in November and again in December because the Republicans and the Democrats couldn't agree on a budget. Then in December Marin County underwent another horrendous series of storms, which caused even more damage and power outages than the ones in the previous winter. And in March another major storm system roared through the area with gale force winds, creating more havoc and causing power outages that lasted in some towns for days (and incited a lot of grumbling toward PG&E).

It remains to be seen whether these "hundred year storms" (as the one in 1982 was labeled) continue to show up once or more per decade—or even per year! Visitors to West Marin should be aware that during severe storms any of the access roads may be closed by floods, slides, or downed trees. To find out the road situation call Caltrans at (800) 427-7623 or (415) 557-3755.

# Plants

Because the rocks of the Point Reyes peninsula differ so markedly from those to the east of the fault zone, it follows that the soils differ also; so it comes as no surprise that the peninsula's plant life differs from that of the mainland.

The majestic Black Forest of Douglas fir on Inverness Ridge is awesomely impressive. John Thomas Howell, the pre-eminent Marin botanist, believed it resembles the dense fir forests of the Pacific Northwest more closely than it does the nearby ones. Another noteworthy conifer is the bishop pine, the only pine native to Marin County. (You will find other pine trees growing in the county—in particular, Monterey pine—but they or their seeds originally came from somewhere else.) Although the bishop occurs sparsely elsewhere in Marin, there were large groves of it on the north end of Inverness Ridge. It is a closed-cone pine: the cones open only after a fire to reseed the forest.

The Vision Fire of October 1995 ripped through many of the bishop pines of Inverness Ridge. According to witnesses, the sound of the cones popping open was like a series of explosions. These were mostly mature trees, because there had not been a fire through this area for almost seven decades. A few months after the fire, young pines were already beginning to reforest the ridge.

Interestingly enough, the coast redwood, which plays such a prominent arboreal role on the east side of the fault zone, is not found on the Point Reyes peninsula. Apparently coast redwoods do not favor granitic soil.

Other trees that occur in association with the Douglas firs and bishop pines are such common central California natives as the coast live oak, the bay, the madrone, and the buckeye.

Your walks in the National Seashore will take you to many kinds of landscapes other than forests: grassy meadows; coastal scrub (also called soft chaparral); marshes, both fresh-water and salt-water; and of course miles of beach and dune. Each of these has its own plant community, and a few of the plants are found only on the Point Reyes peninsula.

From about February through June, all of the landscapes are brightened by the blooming of wildflowers. In the forest the delicate white milkmaids herald the coming of spring. On the coastal bluffs the baby-blue-eyes, pale suncups, shiny buttercups, and elegant iris form a living Oriental carpet thrown over the land. And everywhere the variously colored lupine and the golden California poppy (our state flower) enliven the roadsides. Among the best places to see spring wildflowers are Chimney Rock, Abbotts Lagoon, and Tomales Point.

*Towering Douglas firs and bay trees line the trail*

One plant the Point Reyes peninsula has, alas, in common with much of the rest of northern California—poison oak. It is easy to avoid on the broad and well-traveled trails like Bear Valley, but on narrower and less-frequented trails one should remain alert for the distinctive

*The one plant you must be able to recognize: poison oak*

leaves in groups of three that are glossy green in spring and brilliant red in late summer and fall. It is especially sneaky when encountered as a vine at head level above the trail, often camouflaged by other, harmless plants. If you try going cross-country or on unmaintained trails in brushy areas, be prepared to run into lots of poison oak, and dress accordingly: long pants and long sleeves.

Another annoying plant to avoid is the stinging nettle. Fortunately its effects are not as long-lasting as poison oak's.

Marin supervisors are taking the offensive against aggressive non-native plants which have invaded the county, including parts of the National Seashore, and which are threatening the survival of native species. The most notorious of these are pampas grass, French and Scotch broom, and gorse. If you want to get rid of your aggressions in a socially positive way, ask the Bear Valley Visitor Center when they plan a broom-bashing party! Some native-plant purists would put blue-gum eucalyptus (imported from Australia in the late 19th century) in the same category, but these trees are by now such a prominent part of the historic landscape—for example, along sections of Highway 1—that it would be difficult to eradicate them. Drawings of some of the common flowers of Point Reyes are at the end of this book.

### Recommended reading:

Ferris, Roxana S., *Flowers of Point Reyes National Seashore.* Berkeley, Los Angeles, and London: University of California Press, 1970. Illustrated by Jeanne R. Janish. Paperback.

Howell, John Thomas., *Marin Flora.* 2nd ed. Berkeley and Los Angeles: University of California Press, 1970. Photographs by Charles T. Townsend. First paperback ed., 1985. The definitive guide to the county's plants.

# Birds

The Point Reyes peninsula is a favored haunt of birders, boasting as it does over 400 recorded species. This avian abundance is due partly to the diversity of its habitats—forest, pasture, seashore, marshland, all in close proximity—and partly to its coastal location, which attracts many wintering migrants.

For the casual visitor, perhaps the most exciting bird-oriented activity is watching hawks perched on the fences and telephone poles along the outer stretches of Sir Francis Drake Highway and Pierce Point Road. You can get surprisingly close to these birds, and I have seen drivers almost go off the road when fascinated by a majestic marsh hawk alighting nearby.

The Audubon Society conducts a Christmas count of birds at Point Reyes every year. In recent years as many as 200 birders have shown up, and the number of species identified has ranged between 195 and 200.

One bird that has made a comeback from the endangered species list since DDT was banned in 1972 is the magnificent osprey, or fish hawk. Tomales Bay seems to provide a plentiful source of food for these large birds. They build huge nests atop snags or poles. One pair built a nest on a PG&E power pole on the east side of Tomales Bay which shorted out two wires and caused a temporary power shortage in Inverness. PG&E, at considerable expense, removed the nest to a new pole nearby, and the ospreys settled in. You can see the nest at Alan Sieroty State Beach (p. 101).

Birders were electrified in January 1987 when word got out that a Siberian brown shrike had showed up at Tomales Bay near Point Reyes Station. This carnivorous bird had never been sighted before on the continental mainland of the United States. Apparently it lost its bearings crossing the Bering Strait and migrated down the west coast of America instead of the east coast of the USSR. Dedicated birders reportedly flew in from as far as North Carolina to add the brown shrike to their life lists. Jim Scanlon, in a sardonic column in the Bolinas *Coastal Post*, remarked how fortunate the bird was to have arrived at Tomales Bay rather than reclusive Bolinas—where it might have been kidnapped or *worse*, to prevent hordes of camera-toting birders from descending upon that xenophobic community.

**Cormorants nest on the secluded cliffs near Miller Point**

The NPS conducts frequent guided bird walks; you can get their schedules from the visitor centers. Serious birders will want to visit the Point Reyes Bird Observatory (see p. 96).

### Recommended reading:

Stallcup, Rich, *Field Checklist of Birds: Point Reyes National Seashore*. Point Reyes National Seashore Association, 1992. Available for a very modest price at the visitor centers.

# Land animals

It is evident from travelers' reports that game was once abundant on the peninsula. Drake's annalist remarked on the "herds of wild deer" and the "multitude of a strange kind of Conies," with bags under their chin on either side, which the crew of the *Golden Hinde* encountered. The "deer" were probably tule elk. The "Conies" are somewhat harder to identify with certainty and have burrowed their way into the ongoing Drake controversy. Proponents of Drakes Bay as the *Golden Hinde*'s harbor claim they were pocket gophers, which are indeed multitudinous on the Point Reyes peninsula; proponents of other bays claim they were ground squirrels.

The vaqueros of the early 19th century hunted deer and elk that roamed the peninsula in huge herds. As late as the 1890s the sportsmen of the Pacific Union Club were hunting coyote, bear, and mountain lion, as well as deer and elk in Bear Valley.

Mammals whose tracks, scats, and burrows the modern-day hiker may see include skunks, foxes, bobcats, gophers, weasels, and rabbits. Point Reyes is also the southern limit of the range of a burrowing animal, the *Aplodontia* (called "mountain beaver," although it is not a beaver, but a primitive rodent), which is so reclusive that it is rarely encountered. The *Aplodontia*'s ranks were apparently severely diminished by the fire of 1995, probably because their burrows were not particularly deep; also, they require a constant supply of water. Most of the larger mammals were able to outrun the fire.

An animal you are only too likely to encounter if you are backpacking is the raccoon, which will try to steal your food unless you hang it carefully on the poles provided at the campsites.

Because many ranchers have long-term leases, hikers will continue to see dairy cattle. You may also see a llama or two: Camelid Capers (669-1523) leads llama pack trips in the National Seashore.

By far the most complete account of animal life in West Marin is Jules Evens's *Natural History*, recommended above under "GEOLOGY." Here is a rundown on a few species that have been in the news recently.

## Coyotes

Beginning in the early 1980s a population boom took place among West Marin's coyotes. This proliferation is causing much grief to the sheep ranchers, who are losing more animals every year. In addition to employing a trapper, ranchers have tried using guard animals, including dogs, donkeys, and llamas. One ingenious rancher hooked a radio up in his pasture and found that the sheep were fascinated by the voice of Howard Cosell. None of these attempts has so far been very successful in thwarting the predators.

## Mountain lion *(alias cougar, puma)*

There have probably always been a few mountain lions on the Point Reyes Peninsula since the Seashore was established, but they were rarely sighted because they are usually very shy animals and try to avoid humans. From 1907 until 1933 California had a bounty on mountain lions. In 1990 the state's voters passed an initiative, Proposition 117, protecting the lions except where they were an immediate danger to humans or domestic animals. In recent years the lion population has apparently burgeoned, and the human population of lion habitats has increased. In

1994 a woman runner was killed by a mountain lion in the Sierra Nevada foothills—the first such kill in over 80 years. Subsequently a woman birder was killed in a state park near San Diego. There has also been a rising number of lion attacks on domestic animals in California. In 1995 an initiative (Proposition 197) authorizing sport hunting of cougars made the ballot and caused vociferous arguments among voters. In the primary of March 1996 it was defeated. However, the hunting lobby will probably continue to try to get such a measure passed.

It is most unlikely that you will encounter a mountain lion on the trails of Point Reyes. Tom Stienstra, outdoors columnist for the *San Francisco Examiner*, wrote (April 30, 1995) that in 10,000 miles of hiking he had seen only three. One of these was on Tomales Point; after staring at him for 40 seconds, the lion slunk off and disappeared. As Stienstra points out,

> Encounters with wildlife of even the most menacing reputations, such as mountain lions, grizzly bears, and wild boar, almost always turn out to be far less perilous than the average commute to work. The most dangerous part of outdoor adventures is the act of driving to them.

In case you should encounter a cougar, some authorities recommend the following: keep children close to you; stand up straight and try to look as large as possible; act aggressive—yell, wave your arms; do not run, crouch down, or bend over.

## Deer

It is almost impossible to hike for an hour or so on Point Reyes without seeing a deer. In addition to the native black-tailed deer, the peninsula contains two exotic species: the white-to-brown fallow deer, native to the Mediterranean lands and Asia Minor, and the spotted axis deer, native to India and Ceylon. Both species were introduced to the peninsula in the 1940s and '50s by ranch-owner Dr. Millard Ottinger. The exotic deer flourished in their new habitat, and the herds increased from a few dozen to the hundreds. The three species coexist peacefully but do not interbreed. Ranchers occasionally hunted deer on their own lands, but when the National Seashore was established, hunting was forbidden.

There are not enough mountain lions or other predators in the park to keep the deer population down, and the resulting increase in their numbers presents the NPS with a vexing problem. The Advisory Commission has advised the

*White fallow deer, native to the Mediterranean, were introduced on Point Reyes by a 1940s landowner*

park to keep each of the exotic species down to 350 animals. Some purists want to remove the exotic deer entirely. Some hunters would like to see the park authorize supervised hunting; however, the NPS takes a dim view of this proposal in an area that attracts over two million visitors a year. Some animal-rights activists just want to leave all the deer alone. Meanwhile, NPS rangers cull the herds annually and donate some of the venison to St. Anthony's Dining Room in San Francisco and, occasionally, to Native American ceremonies in Mendocino County.

I personally enjoy sighting the white deer. Even purists acknowledge that it is impossible to eliminate all the non-native animals in the park. According to David Rolland, writing in the *Point Reyes Light* of December 8, 1994, these include: cattle, feral pigs, feral dogs, feral cats, feral goats, red foxes, muskrats, porcupines (apparently), possums, several varieties of oyster, peacocks, starlings, and cowbirds.

A modest proposal appeared subsequently as a letter to the editor (December 22, 1994):

> To the Editor:
> In the David Rolland article on culling axis and fallow deer, there was an extensive listing of other non-native species proliferating in West Marin.
> However, there was a significant omission, namely, the European and other non-native homo sapiens species. If these could be culled, then one could begin to restore a proper ecological balance by re-introducing original native species such as bears and bunch grass.
> Unfortunately it may be very difficult to find original pure bred strains of native homo sapiens for restocking.
> —— John Gibson, Oakland

## Elk

The last of the Point Reyes tule elk were slaughtered for their meat and hides in the 1860s—unless, as one report had it, they swam to safety across Tomales Bay. In 1978 the National Park Service reintroduced a small herd transported from the Owens Valley in Southern California. The elk are fenced off in 2,600 acres on the northern part of Tomales Point.

The original herd of 13 has flourished to the point that it now numbers over 200. The Park Service began to worry that the elk, like the exotic deer, might overpopulate their habitat. A panel of experts decided that the carrying capacity of Pierce Point is probably as high as 350 elk, so for the present the NPS need not make a decision on culling the herd. Possibly the population will self-regulate, or possibly the resurgence of coyotes and mountain lions will cull the herd without human intervention.

## Ticks

In the past decade one animal has progressed from being a mere annoyance to an actual danger: the Western black-legged tick. A small percentage of these ticks—probably less than five percent—carry the spirochete that causes Lyme disease (named for Old Lyme, Connecticut, where it was first diagnosed in 1975).

Symptoms can include a red, circular rash and/or a fever, followed by neurological and/or cardiac problems and arthritis-like joint pains. Drugs are effective against Lyme disease once it is correctly diagnosed.

The best way to avoid Lyme disease is to avoid ticks. Apply insect repellent before going outdoors. Wear light-colored clothing so that ticks will be more easily visible; wear long sleeves and long pants. Because ticks generally travel upward, tuck pants into socks and tuck shirts into pants. If you find a tick on you, try to get someone else to remove it with tweezers as soon as possible.

### Recommended reading

> Drummond, Roger, *Ticks and What You Can Do About Them.* Berkeley: Wilderness Press, 1990.

# Aquatic animals

## Seals

The National Seashore has the largest breeding colony of harbor seals in the state. You will frequently see them hauled out on the beaches of the esteros and Tomales Bay. Note that harbor-seal mothers may leave their pups on the beach while they search for food. If you come upon a lonesome seal pup, don't assume it has been abandoned and *don't move it*. Harbor seals are very sensitive to any disturbance from people , dogs, or boats. If you think you see a seal in distress, tell a ranger or call the Marine Mammal Center's 24-hour rescue line at 289-SEAL.

Note that the Marine Mammal Protection Act of 1972 prohibits "harassment" of these animals, which is defined as any human action that causes a change in the behavior of a marine mammal. The Seashore recommends maintaining a distance of 100 yards from all marine mammals.

Elephant seals, once nearly extinct, have made an amazing comeback since the Mexican and US governments started protecting them in the 1920s. The most visible colony in northern California is at Año Nuevo in San Mateo County. Another colony established itself on the Farallones in the 1970s, and a small colony on a secluded beach at Point Reyes in the 1980s. The storms of 1995 apparently caused some of the elephant seals to relocate to Drakes Bay. In April 1995 Park

*Steller's sea lions often haul out on the ocean side of Tomales Point*

Superintendent Neubacher, addressing the West Marin Chamber of Commerce, noted that although it is encouraging to see this species making a comeback, if the giant animals take to hanging out regularly at Drakes Beach, some means may have to be devised to regulate human/seal interaction, as has been done at Año Nuevo.

By 1996 the elephant seal colony at Point Reyes was estimated at over a thousand animals. The males arrive in December and the breeding season lasts from January through March. Park visitors should remember to keep their distance from the elephant seals, which can weigh well over a ton and can move astonishingly quickly if disturbed.

## Whales

By far the most spectacular marine mammals visible in the National Seashore are not residents but migrants: the California gray whales that travel from Alaska to Baja California every winter, returning north in spring. These magnificent animals often pass within a few hundred yards of the coast. On a clear day the lucky visitor may see dozens of whales, and may even see them "breach"—leap out of the water as high as 30 feet.

The whales begin to appear off the Sonoma and Marin coasts in December and January. The first to migrate are the pregnant females, traveling to the warmer waters of Baja to give birth to their young. They are followed by courting males and females and finally by juveniles. The return north begins in mid-February, the mothers and their calves bringing up the rear. March and April are the best times to view the returning whales.

The gray whale was hunted nearly to extinction until an international treaty in 1946 put it under protection. In 1970 it was covered under the US Endangered Species Act. By 1994 the gray whale had made such a successful comeback that it was removed from the list of endangered species. Current estimates place the population at about 21,000.

The best places to watch the whales are from the lighthouse area and the western cliffs and beaches. Whale watching has become so popular that the park has instituted a free shuttle bus between South Beach and the lighthouse to avoid traffic jams on the narrow road. To find out in advance about weather conditions, whale activity, traffic, etc., you can call Bear Valley headquarters (663-1092) or the lighthouse visitor center (669-1534).

## Fish and shellfish

The best way to find out about fishing possibilities and regulations in the National Seashore is to pick up a free information sheet on the subject at the Bear Valley Visitor Center. A few pointers to bear in mind:

Persons 16 years of age or older must have in their possession a valid California state fishing license for the taking of any kind of fish, mollusk, invertebrate, amphibian, crustacean, or reptile (except for rattlesnakes). All anglers are responsible for adhering to all fishing hours, limits, methods, and other regulations found in the pamphlet *California Sport Fishing Regulations*, obtainable at stores selling fishing licenses, bait, and equipment. You should obtain your fishing license *be-*

*fore* you come to the park. The visitor centers provide maps showing fishing areas and restricted areas within the Seashore.

The surf on the ocean beaches is extremely hazardous.

Mussels are quarantined every year from May 1 to November 1 because they may be poisonous then. The poison results from shellfish consuming toxic algae, the "red tides" of summer and early fall.

## Sharks

Great white sharks inhabit the waters off the coast. In fact, shark expert John McCosker of Steinhart Aquarium at the California Academy of Sciences has christened the oceanic area between Año Nuevo, the Farallon Islands, and Tomales Bay the "Red Triangle"—one of the world's prime spots for shark attacks. He noted that by 1993 there had been 69 shark attacks on humans along the California coast, of which 8 were fatal. Probably the sharks are attracted to the area by the increasing population of seals and sea lions, their favorite dinner.

To avoid a shark attack:

- Don't go out too far; most attacks have been at least 200 yards from shore.
- Don't go out alone; many people who were bitten were saved by their companions.
- Don't swim or dive near Bird Rock, off Tomales Point; this appears to be a prime hangout for great white sharks.

## Oysters

Tomales Bay is still one of the least polluted estuaries on the Pacific Coast—although this situation may change if development takes place along the eastern shore. At present it is an excellent place for growing oysters. A drive north from Point Reyes Station along Highway 1 will take you past the Tomales Bay Oyster Company (663-1242) and the Hog Island Oyster Company (663-9218). You will also pass two popular seafood restaurants, Tony's (663-1107) and Nick's (663-1033). In fact, most of the restaurants in the Point Reyes area serve oysters.

A long-time favorite among lovers of the succulent bivalve is Johnson's Oyster Farm on Drakes Bay; it is described on pp. 68–70.

# History

The first residents of Point Reyes were Coast Miwok Indians. Archeologists have identified 113 aboriginal village sites on the peninsula; indeed, probably more people were living there in the 16th century than there are in the 20th. With bow and arrow they hunted deer, elk, bear, and mountain lion. They also gathered clams and mussels, and in small canoes made of rushes they fished the bays. A peaceable people, they greeted the first European visitors—Drake and Cermeño—with friendliness.

When the Franciscan fathers established Mission San Rafael in 1817, they recruited the Point Reyes Indians, converted them, and persuaded them to take up agriculture. Many of the Indians died of the white man's diseases, particularly smallpox. When the Mexican government secularized the missions in the 1830s, the Indian proselytes were left to fend for themselves, and many starved. A culture that had existed for hundreds of years in ecological harmony with its land thus perished in only one generation. However, you can get some idea of how the Point Reyes Indians lived when you visit Kule Loklo, the reconstructed Miwok Village near park headquarters (see p. 43).

The first European to set foot on the peninsula was probably Francis Drake, in 1579—although after 400 years debate still rages fiercely on this matter (see pp. 72–76).

The first of 40 recorded shipwrecks in the area was that of Sebastian Rodriguez Cermeño's *San Agustin* in 1595. The Portuguese captain was bringing a Manila galleon laden with luxury cargo—including silks and porcelain—from the Philippines to Acapulco. The Spanish government in Mexico had also commissioned him to explore the California coast in search of suitable harbors for the galleons. Cermeño brought the *San Agustin* into Drakes Bay to reconnoiter. (He called it the Bay of San Francisco, thereby adding to the eventual confusion attending the identification and nomenclature of the various ports along the coast.) While most of the crew was ashore, a sudden gale dashed the galleon onto the shore and wrecked her, killing several of the men. The cargo was lost; the local Indians later collected bits and pieces of the priceless Ming porcelain that washed ashore, which archaeologists subsequently discovered when they excavated Miwok villages.

Cermeño salvaged a small open launch, the *San Buenaventura*, and with his 70 remaining men and a dog set out in it for home. After a grueling voyage that represents one of the most remarkable feats of seamanship on record, they arrived safely in Mexico in January of 1596—except for the dog, which the men ate when they got desperate.

In the spring of 1995 a team of students from Sonoma State University, accompanied by members of the Drake Navigators Guild and NPS staff, started an archeological search for the site of Cermeño's camp. As this book goes to press, they have not found anything except some fragments from World War II test bombings, but they may continue searching. No one involved expects to find any treasure, because the sailors would have taken any non-breakable valuables with them, but it would be fascinating to locate the exact site of the shipwreck of a Manila galleon.

*The Drake Navigators Guild has commemorated the entrance to Drake's Estero, where it believes he landed in 1579*

Seven years after the *San Buenaventura* returned to Mexico, one of the survivors, Sebastian Vizcaino, sailed back up the California coast. He arrived off the peninsula on January 6, 1603, the Day of the Three Kings, and christened it *Punto de los Reyes*.

Point Reyes was part of Alta California, a Spanish colony, but the Spaniards never settled the peninsula. After Mexico threw off the Spanish yoke in 1821, the Mexican government began handing out land grants in California on a lavish scale. In 1836 James R. Berry, an Irishman who had served as a colonel in the Mexican army, was awarded about 35,000 acres in the northern part of the Olema Valley—Rancho Punta de los Reyes. In the same year Rafael Garcia was granted nearly 9,000 acres on the southern part of the peninsula—Rancho Tomales y Baulenes. Even by the rather lax standards of land stewardship prevailing at the time, both men were remarkably casual about their holdings. Berry sold part of his land (though sale was forbidden by the terms of his grant), and hired Garcia to run cattle on part of the rest; and Garcia let his brother-in-law move into part of his share. As Marin historian Jack Mason put it: "By 1844 nobody seemed to know who owned what, and the rancheros asked Monterey [the capital of Alta California] to straighten things out. Whatever progress they may have made was wiped out in the American conquest of California in 1846." After decades of tangled litigation, most of the peninsula ended up in the hands of three lawyers from Vermont: brothers Oscar L. Shafter and James McMillan Shafter, and Charles Webb Howard, who married Oscar Shafter's daughter.

In the late 1850s the Shafter-Howard clan began leasing the land for dairy farming—a use that continues to this day. Point Reyes butter was of the highest quality, and was preferred by such elegant customers as San Francisco's Palace Hotel. Schooners carrying butter and live hogs traveled once or twice a week from Drakes Estero to the City, returning with feed and grain.

In the 1860s the Shafter-Howard group designated their dairy ranches by the letters of the alphabet, beginning with A at the lighthouse and proceeding clockwise around the peninsula to Z Ranch on Mt. Wittenberg. NPS Historian Dewey Livingston has spent years researching the history of these ranches and has written a monumental study on the subject, *Ranching on the Point Reyes Peninsula: A History of the Dairy and Beef Ranches Within Point Reyes National Seashore, 1834–1992*. The NPS issued this book in a very limited edition; there are copies of it in West Marin libraries, and anyone who is seriously interested in the subject can refer to it at Seashore headquarters.

To visit the sites of the early dairies, try the hike on pp. 61–64. For a good illustration of how the ranches operated, visit the restored Pierce Point Ranch (pp. 88).

A wagon road from San Rafael to Olema was completed in 1867, and thereafter a stagecoach made the trip twice a week. The town of Olema flourished, at one point boasting three hotels. James M. Shafter thought a railroad from the eastern part of the county would be a profitable venture, and he invested heavily in the North Pacific Coast Railroad. The first train ran from Sausalito to Tomales in 1875. However, far from enriching Shafter, the railroad threatened to bankrupt him.

In an attempt to pay off his creditors—who included Leland Stanford and Wells Fargo—he created the town of Inverness in 1889 on 640 acres of his land on the western shore of Tomales Bay. He also envisioned an even grander development on the shore of Drakes Bay. But before these plans could come to fruition, Shafter died. His three children, especially his daughter Julia, struggled for most of their lives to pay off his debts. San Francisco's exclusive Pacific Union Club in

1895 bought 110 acres of their Bear Valley land (for $6,000!) as the site of a country club. Here the cream of San Francisco male society, and such guests as Teddy Roosevelt and Ignace Paderewski, came to hunt the deer, coyote, bear, and mountain lion which still inhabited the peninsula. Julia's attempt to sell her Inverness lots was thwarted by the earthquake of 1906, which severely damaged several buildings in the village.

During Prohibition, the isolated and sparsely inhabited peninsula was a natural location for extensive rum-running and bootlegging. The multitude of bay and ocean beaches and of private wharves facilitated transfer of the liquor from ships standing offshore, down from Canada. Many—probably most—of the ranchers were more sympathetic to the bootleggers than to the Prohibition agents, and looked the other way when they heard trucks roaring over the back roads at midnight.

Shortly before World War II the last of the Shafter-Howard properties was sold off. The San Francisco investor who bought Oscar's heirs' land almost immediately resold it at a profit. The Los Angeles syndicate that bought most of James Shafter's son's property announced grandiose plans for it, as had James earlier: formation of deluxe villa sites, a polo ground, a golf course, and other expensive amenities. The war put an end to these dreams, at least temporarily.

# The making of a park

As early as 1935 the National Park Service had recommended the purchase of 53,000 acres of Point Reyes for $2.4 million, or about $45 per acre. In retrospect this seems an incredible bargain, but at that time the country was still staggering out of the Great Depression, and Congress did not throw around huge sums with carefree abandon.

Meanwhile, Marin conservationists succeeded in having a few properties set aside as county parks: a parcel at Drakes Beach in 1938 and at McClures Beach in 1942 (both of which were subsequently taken over by the National Seashore), and the nucleus of Tomales Bay State Park in 1945.

After World War II the National Park Service began studying Point Reyes with increasingly urgent interest. For a century, various landowners and promoters had talked of exploiting this land and subdividing it for estates, but somehow their plans had always come to nothing. Now, however, loggers were actually cutting down trees on Inverness Ridge, and surveyors were actually marking off lots above Limantour Spit. At this point Marin conservationists gained a powerful ally—Clem Miller, the new Congressman from the district in which Point Reyes lay. California Senator Clair Engle also took a keen interest in the proposed park. Opposition came not only from developers but also from ranch owners who wanted to go on following their traditional way of life. Extensive negotiations made it possible for them to continue ranching on long-term leases. In 1962 President John F. Kennedy signed the Point Reyes National Seashore Bill authorizing the original 53,000 acres.

Congress, however, was niggardly in appropriating funds for purchasing the land. The original $13 million authorized ran out before half of the 53,000 acres

**A row of houses once lined Limantour Spit in the background**

were acquired, and as land values in Marin escalated in the following years the National Park Service was often just one jump ahead of the developers. The final cost of the park was $56 million—more than four times the amount initially budgeted. The National Park Service learned a valuable, albeit expensive, lesson from this experience.

As John Hart points out in *San Francisco's Wilderness Next Door*, the delay in completing the park led to one providential and incalculable benefit. In the early '60s most planners as well as the general public thought of parks in terms of organized and *motorized* recreation. Point Reyes National Seashore was originally planned to accommodate motor boats, dune buggies, campers, trailers, and of course thousands of cars. But by the time the last of the originally planned land was acquired in 1972, northern Californians had begun to rebel against the tyranny of the internal-combustion engine. Now they wanted to preserve the peninsula in as near its natural state as possible, as a unique heritage from the past.

The only major construction that resulted from the planners' original auto-oriented outlook is the broad northern section of the Limantour Road, which was authorized along its present route in 1966. Construction within a 400-foot right-of-way in steep terrain necessitated much cut and fill, and evoked howls from environmentalists. The National Park Service's money ran out before the road could be completed on the grandiose scale originally planned, and therefore it reverts abruptly near its summit to the original narrow paving. As it turned out, the opponents of the Limantour Road were vindicated in January 1982, when a monumental rainstorm washed out a large part of the new section and the road had to be closed for a year.

Another reason Point Reyes National Seashore developed differently in the 1970s than might have been expected in the early '60s is that when the Golden

*Dorothy Whitnah*

***The Upper Pierce Ranch buildings on Tomales Point are being maintained by the National Park Service***

Gate National Recreation Area was established in 1972 it became natural to regard the peninsula as the northernmost and least developed part of a greenbelt of over 100,000 acres—an unprecedented stretch of parkland in and near a major metropolitan center. The Advisory Commission that was established in 1972 to oversee the development of the GGNRA also looks after adjoining Point Reyes. This Commission meets regularly at various places in the Bay Area, and welcomes suggestions and opinions from the public. (To find out the schedule of meetings, phone 556-4484.)

Beginning in 1975 the National Park Service held over 200 workshops among various Bay Area community groups to find out what the public wanted from the two parks. Some parts of the GGNRA, such as Alcatraz, stirred up considerable controversy; but there was general agreement that Point Reyes should be left substantially as it was.

# Preserving the park

Some of the park has not only been left as it was in 1970, but is being encouraged to revert to an earlier state: in 1976 Congress designated 32,000 acres as wilderness or potential wilderness (no permanent structures or major roads, no motorized vehicles allowed except for emergencies). In 1985 the designated wilderness area of the Seashore was officially dedicated to Congressman Phillip Burton, who had died in 1983. Burton, Representative from San Francisco since 1964, was responsible for more than doubling the wilderness acreage in the national-park system. Congress chose Point Reyes to commemorate him because it was the wilderness area closest to his home.

Another 18,000 acres are zoned for ranching on long-term lease, because the National Park Service believes that on these lands "dairying and cattle ranching are desirable aspects of the scene from both an educational and esthetic point of view."

That ranching can continue in the National Seashore and surrounding areas is due to an unusual turnaround in public policy that took place in the 1960s and '70s. In the early 1960s nearly all county officials assumed that West Marin would inevitably become urbanized, necessitating (or encouraged by) a giant freeway from San Rafael to Point Reyes Station. But in 1971 the supervisors presented the public with a new plan that limited urbanization to the eastern part of the county. In 1972 the supervisors voted for A-60 zoning in West Marin—that is, zoning for a 60-acre minimum parcel—which they figured would help maintain agricultural use of the land and hinder developers from breaking it up into "ranchettes." A Chicago developer who owned 561 acres in Nicasio that he wanted to subdivide fought the county's zoning unsuccessfully for years, all the way up to the US Supreme Court—which refused to hear his case.

In 1980 environmentalists and ranchers combined to form the Marin Agricultural Land Trust (MALT) as an additional incentive to preserve ranching in the county. MALT's program is to buy easements from ranch owners that will keep the property permanently in agriculture, even if it subsequently passes into other hands. This easement not only provides the landowners with immediate cash but also lowers the tax rate on the land, since it can no longer be developed. By its 15th year in operation MALT had secured easements on over 25,000 acres. The whole notion of such farmland trusts started here, and one of the founders of MALT, Ralph Grossi, has gone on to head the American Farmland Trust.

Meanwhile, the GGNRA has acquired some small parcels on the east side of Tomales Bay (see pp. 100–01) that are open to the public, and some large parcels in the Lagunitas Loop (east of Highway 1 and north of Sir Francis Drake Highway) that are not yet open to public access.

In 1992 West Marin county supervisor Gary Giacomini, who has been a tireless champion of preserving agriculture and open space, proposed a plan whereby the federal government in partnership with MALT would procure easements on 40,000 acres of land on the east shore of Tomales Bay. In 1994 Marin Representative Lynn Woolsey prepared a bill to this effect, but it died without coming to a vote in the House. Then came the election of the 104th Congress, which so far has taken a notably parsimonious attitude toward national parks. Now . . . MALT is run-

**On the Olema Valley Trail**

*Dorothy Whitnah*

ning low on funds; and supervisor Giacomini, after 24 years on the board, decided not to run again for re-election.

## Offshore oil

On October 31, 1984, the tanker *Puerto Rican* exploded off the Golden Gate. As the ship was being towed out to sea, it broke in two. The bow half was towed to Richmond, but the stern half, containing 1.5 million gallons of oil, sank under 2,400 feet of water about 26 miles off Half Moon Bay, on the edge of the Point Reyes-Farallon Islands Marine Sanctuary (since rechristened the Gulf of the Farallones National Marine Sanctuary). Leaking oil was carried by ocean currents and storms to the Farallones and the mainland coast as far north as Bodega Bay, killing thousands of waterfowl.

In November 1986 the owners of the *Puerto Rican* offered $1.7 million in settlement to state and federal agencies for damages and clean-up costs—not as much as originally claimed, but, as a deputy attorney general involved in the case noted, damages to the environment are difficult to quantify. This compensation was based partly on the estimated monetary value of 2,874 seabirds killed by the spill.

The *Puerto Rican* oil spill intensified coastal dwellers' concern over possible offshore drilling. Every Secretary of the Interior under the Reagan administration sought to lease tracts off the California coast for oil and gas drilling, despite vociferous opposition from environmentalists, the fishing industry, and other coastal businesses.

The Department of the Interior in February 1988 held hearings in Eureka and Fort Bragg on plans to lease over a million acres off the coasts of Humboldt and Mendocino counties and to install as many as 24 giant oil rigs. These hearings drew such huge, impassioned, noisy crowds of drilling opponents that then-Interior Secretary Hodel—bowing to politics in an election year—put all such plans on the shelf until the next administration.

President George Bush in 1990 pledged to remove parts of the national coastline from oil drilling, and in 1994 Republican Governor Pete Wilson signed a bill to ban drilling all along the California coast within the 3-mile limit. In 1995 a House subcommittee of the Republican-controlled 104th Congress voted to allow drilling in federal waters, which extend from 3 miles to 200 miles offshore. Subsequently, however, Republicans from coastal states joined Democrats on the House Appropriations Committee in reversing the subcommittee's decision.

Since 1981 the waters off Point Reyes have been part of the Gulf of the Farallones National Marine Sanctuary, encompassing 948 square nautical miles from Bodega Bay to Bolinas and including the Farallon Islands National Wildlife Refuge. In 1989 President Bush and Congress authorized the 397-square-mile Cordell Bank National Marine Sanctuary off the coast of Point Reyes. (The Cordell Bank is an underwater mountain about 20 miles offshore which is home to a wide variety of marine life.) Drilling and mineral exploration are banned in the sanctuaries, but these are not protected from oil spills from tankers operating beyond their boundaries. And of course what Congress hath given Congress can always take away—although if it tried to desanctify these waters the political fallout in California would be horrendous.

## Buck Trust

Visitors to the National Seashore will occasionally come across plaques noting that certain facilities—e.g., the Bear Valley Visitor Center—were made possible with the help of a grant from the San Francisco Foundation, the Marin Community Foundation, or the Buck Trust (or Fund). These reflect one of the more bizarre chapters in the history of organized philanthropy.

In 1975 Beryl Buck, a childless widow, died and in her will specified that the yearly earnings from her estate were to be used "for exclusively nonprofit, charitable, religious, or educational purposes in providing care for the needy of Marin, and for other nonprofit, charitable, religious, or educational purposes of that county." To administer it, Mrs. Buck appointed the San Francisco Foundation, a hitherto low-key institution accustomed to distributing philanthropic monies around the Bay Area. By the time her estate was settled, her original bequest of a comparatively modest $7 million in oil stock had ballooned to over $250 million, meaning that the San Francisco Foundation now had $20 million or more to distribute every year in what was already one of the wealthiest counties in California.

The San Francisco Foundation, abetted by a group of public-interest lawyers representing other Bay Area charities, petitioned to break the "Marin-only" feature of Mrs. Buck's will. They were opposed by the Marin Board of Supervisors, the Marin Council of Agencies, and Mrs. Buck's attorney. The resulting bitter court fight was dubbed "The Superbowl of Probate."

Ultimately in 1986 the San Francisco Foundation not only had to give up its attempt to break Mrs. Buck's will, but also agreed to turn over the giant trust to a

*The Point Reyes Headlands*

Paul Backhurst

new, Marin-based foundation. Ironically enough, over $10 million of Mrs. Buck's estate—which, remember, was originally intended for "the needy of Marin"—went to lawyers for both sides.

This settlement, however, did not end the controversy over the Buck Trust. The presiding judge set aside about a quarter of the trust's annual income for three long-term projects: the Beryl Buck Institute for Education; the Marin Institute for Alcohol and Other Drug Problems; and the Buck Center for Research on Aging, which got the lion's share. By 1990, the trust's principal had grown to over $450 million, allowing the Center for Research on Aging about $4.5 million per year. The Center bought almost 500 acres of land near Novato and hired world-famous architect I.M. Pei to design its facilities. Meanwhile, advocates for the truly needy—the homeless, the disabled, the elderly (and there are plenty of these in Marin, despite its high average per-capita wealth)—continued to fight the Center project, pointing out that the millions of dollars that had been spent on a geologically questionable site and on high-priced architects, lawyers, and administrators might better have gone to the poor whom Beryl Buck originally named in her will. Animal-rights groups also objected to the Center's proposed use of animals for research, and environmentalists were concerned about hazardous waste. Nevertheless the county supervisors in 1994 voted 3–2 to approve the project. The opposition immediately started a petition drive to put the issue on the ballot.

In November 1995 the county voted by 52% to reverse the supervisors' vote, even though the Buck Aging Center had reportedly spent over a half million dollars of Buck Trust funds on a campaign to get the voters to approve it. (Remember: Mrs. Buck originally designated her estate to benefit "the needy" of Marin County—in which she probably didn't include public-relations consultants.) The City of Novato, however, where the Center would officially be located, voted in its favor. The resulting controversy, and no doubt litigation, will probably continue.

> Editor:
>     The moral of the Buck Trust: if you plan on leaving pots of money to a cause, make it a super-specific cause, such as for endangered species of newts crossing the road at sunset (going east to west), rather than "for the needy," as the latter is too open for interpretation.
>         Paki Stedwell-Wright, in a letter to the *Pacific Sun*, April 13, 1990.

Despite all this controversy, the Buck Trust has been notably helpful to environmental interests in Marin, contributing not only to the Bear Valley Visitor Center but also to MALT, the Marconi Conference Center, and the Clem Miller Environmental Education Center in the National Seashore.

## New superintendent

In January 1995 John Sansing retired as Superintendent of the National Seashore, having held the post since 1970—longer than any current National Park superintendent. It was a tribute to his administration that Tom Stienstra of the *San Francisco Examiner* in 1993 rated Point Reyes as Number One among Bay Area parks. Sansing was also known as a proponent of maintaining ranching in the

National Seashore and the GGNRA.

To replace Sansing the NPS appointed Don Neubacher, a native of Sonoma County, long a resident of West Marin, and previously for some time chief of interpretation at the National Seashore. This was a popular choice with the locals, who expect that he will maintain good relations with the ranchers. Almost immediately upon taking office, Neubacher was beset by a series of calamities that would have tried the patience of Job. First the storms of early 1995 inflicted hundreds of thousands of dollars of damage on the park. Just as things appeared to be getting back to normal, the Vision Fire of October 1995 burned up about 15% of the park's acreage and forced the closure of many of the roads and trails and two of the camps. While the PRNS staff was trying to cope with this situation, the federal government shut down the entire NPS *twice* because the Republicans and the Democrats couldn't agree on a budget—a week in November and three weeks in December and January. And in the winter and again in March West Marin experienced more storms, even worse than the ones earlier in the year, causing damage to animals, trees, and buildings, and power outages lasting in some areas for days.

Somehow Neubacher remained steadfast in the face of all these tribulations. In March 1996 the Point Reyes Business Association honored him as one of two Citizens of the Year 1995, for "his influence and leadership during the Mt. Vision fire, for his role in promoting visitation of the park following the fire, and for his contributions to the community" (*Point Reyes Light*, March 7, 1996). Later in the year the West Marin Chamber of Commerce chose Neubacher to receive the 1996 "Spirit of Marin" award.

### Recommended reading:

Hart, John, *Farming on the Edge: Saving Family Farms in Marin County, California*. Berkeley, Los Angeles, Oxford: University of California Press, 1991.

Mason, Jack, *Point Reyes, the Solemn Land*. 3rd ed. Inverness: North Shore Books, 1980. The late historian of West Marin wrote several other books, alone and in cooperation with other authors. Some relevant titles are: *Earthquake Bay: A History of Tomales Bay; Last Stage for Bolinas;* and *Summer Town: The History of Inverness, California*.

Thalman, Sylvia Barker, *The Coast Miwok Indians of the Point Reyes Area*. Point Reyes National Seashore Association, 1993.

# Transit

The park planners, both professional and amateur, have devoted an enormous amount of time and energy to the problems involved in getting *to* the park and getting around *in* it. In fact, probably no other issue (except rules governing dogs and bicycles) has evoked so much emotion. The problems are more vexing in Point Reyes than in the GGNRA because the peninsula is farther from San Francisco and from most public transit.

Nearly everyone agrees that people without automobiles—as the late geologist Clyde Wahrhaftig put it, "the large number of my fellow citizens who are too

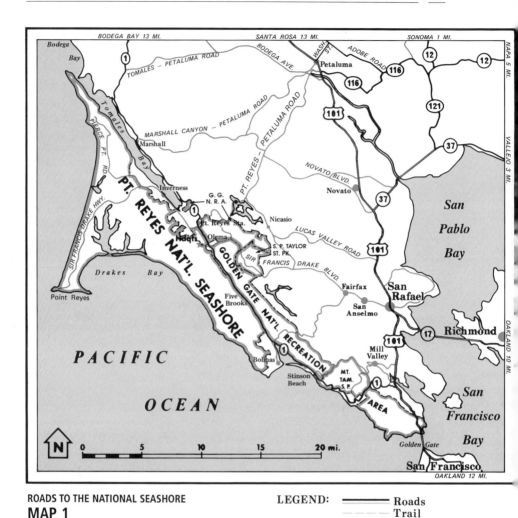

**ROADS TO THE NATIONAL SEASHORE**
**MAP 1**

LEGEND:  ═══════ Roads
         ─ ─ ─ ─ Trail
         ▬▬▬▬ Park Bdy.
         ✪ Campground

old, too young, too poor, or too wise to own a car"—should be able to get to the park. And the residents of the small villages adjoining the park wax vehement against widening the roads to encourage more auto traffic, or building more parking lots near their homes. And anyone who has crept south on Highway 101 toward the Golden Gate Bridge at dusk on a fair Sunday will admit that weekend traffic snarls in Marin County have already reached horrendous proportions.

Conservation activists and the park's managers have propagandized in favor of public transit, and the GGNRA-Point Reyes General Management Plan outlines several proposals relying heavily on buses and ferries.

And yet . . . so far it has seemed almost impossible to pry Americans out of their cars. As the park planners sum it up, the general attitude among the public is, "I want to drive there, but everyone else should take the bus." Bolinas attorney

Paul Kayfetz was equally pessimistic when he testified before the Advisory Commission in October 1979: "If we did everything possible to provide public access to the park, we would be able to, at a maximum, triple the number of visitors coming to the park in buses . . . Only 95 percent of visitors will be coming to the park in autos, instead of 98.5 percent."

The transportation situation may change abruptly, depending on the price and availability of gas, the funding of public transit, and other unpredictables.

## How to get there by bus:

Golden Gate Transit bus #65 runs on Saturdays, Sundays, and holidays from San Rafael to Olema, Point Reyes National Seashore Headquarters, Point Reyes Station, and Inverness. San Rafael is a major transfer point for buses from San Francisco, Sonoma County, and the rest of Marin County.

Because the #65 runs to the Seashore in the morning and returns in the late afternoon, the bus rider can spend most of a day enjoying the park.

For information on schedules and fees, phone Golden Gate Transit:

> from San Francisco, (415) 332-6600;
> from Marin, (415) 453-2100;
> from Sonoma, (707) 544-1323.

## How to get there by car:

There are three principal routes to headquarters at Bear Valley. (For routes to Palomarin, the lighthouse, and the various beaches, see their respective sections.) The quickest is from Highway 101 west on Sir Francis Drake Boulevard (which subsequently becomes Sir Francis Drake Highway) through Samuel P. Taylor State Park to Olema, where signs point the way to park headquarters ½ mile west. A slower, more scenic route from San Francisco or southern Marin is via winding Highway 1 north to Olema. Another scenic route is by Highway 101 and Lucas Valley Road through Nicasio to Point Reyes Station and south to Olema.

During heavy storms, some of these routes may be closed because of flooding or trees blown down on the roads. To find out the conditions, phone Caltrans at (800) 427-7623 or (415) 557-3755.

In the summer of 1988 Caltrans began double-striping roads in West Marin, making it illegal for cars to pass one another on the double-striped sections. This action was the result of a 10-year-old federal order—originally intended as a safety measure—to forbid passing on all two-lane rural highways with visibility of less than a thousand feet. California was the last state to comply with the rule, but finally had to give in under the threat that otherwise the federal government would withhold all highway funds. Caltrans correctly foresaw that residents of rural areas like Big Sur and West Marin would be furious when they found mile after mile of their roads double-striped, with few turnouts. The net result of this supposed safety measure may be *more* accidents, as frustrated drivers caught behind slow-moving vehicles and finding no legal place to pass will dash across the lines into an unsafe place.

Now all the access roads to the National Seashore are double-striped for most of their length. Visitors driving in the area should bear in mind:

1. The fine for crossing a double line is $81 on the first offense;
2. California law requires any slower-moving vehicle closely followed by five or more other vehicles to pull over at the first opportunity.

Caltrans ran into more trouble in West Marin in 1993 when the agency installed a series of emergency call boxes on poles along Highway 1. Residents complained that the boxes were placed on the west side of the highway, where they were bound to spoil views of Bolinas Lagoon and Tomales Bay. After much outcry, and after vandals tore down a few poles, Caltrans relocated some of the most controversial ones.

Then, to placate drivers frustrated by the double-striping on Highway 1, Caltrans constructed 22 turnouts along the road. (A few years earlier, the agency had proposed widening and straightening parts of the highway—but that proposal met with such vociferous opposition from West Marin residents that the agency abandoned the plan.) The turnouts were a good idea, but then Caltrans installed five signs at each one, three of them reading "No Parking." Residents objected that this was overkill and that once again Caltrans was disregarding the scenic values of Highway 1. The agency agreed to remove some of the signs.

As for Bolinas, Caltrans has apparently given up (see p. 39).

## Within the park:

On summer weekends and holidays the park used to provide free shuttle-bus service between Bear Valley headquarters and Limantour. This service was a great boon to hikers and backpackers, making possible one-way, all-downhill trips. However, first the closing of the Limantour Road because of storm damage (see p. 19) and then the greatly reduced NPS budget have eliminated the shuttle bus.

When whale watching became such a popular activity that on weekends cars were lined up for miles along the narrow road to the lighthouse, the Park Service instituted free shuttle-bus service between South Beach and the lighthouse during the height of the whale migration.

# Facilities

The Seashore issues a thrice yearly newsletter which is available free at the visitor centers and which contains all sorts of useful information, including schedules of naturalist activities; phone numbers of restaurants, stores, lodgings, and churches in the area; and a map of the Bear Valley Visitor Center area. Headquarters also has a recorded daily report on weather conditions, campsite availability, and other information at 663-9029.

## Visitor centers

• Headquarters, Bear Valley—8 A.M.–5 P.M. weekends and holidays, 9 A.M.–

5 P.M. weekdays (663-1092).

- Drakes Beach—10 A.M.–5 P.M. weekends and holidays, but closed noon–12:30 P.M. (669-1250).
- Lighthouse—10 A.M.–5 P.M. Thursday through Monday, but closed when very foggy or windy (669-1534).

Address of all of the above: Point Reyes, CA 94956.

*Enjoying a snack at the Drakes Beach visitor center*

## Picnicking

At present the only food concession in the park is at Drakes Beach, open 11:00 A.M.–4:30 P.M. Friday through Tuesday, "weather permitting" (669-1297). It is definitely superior to most food concessions in parks. Several towns adjoining the park have grocery stores, restaurants, and delicatessens where you can buy food for picnicking.

Next to the parking lot near the Bear Valley Visitor Center is a picnic ground with tables but no stoves. All the backpacking camps have picnic tables and braziers; so does Drakes Beach.

## Camping

The only overnight camping in the park is at hike-in camps for backpackers. The Bear Valley Visitor Center will provide visitors with a free list of nearby car-camping facilities. (The nearest are at Olema Ranch Campground and Samuel P. Taylor State Park.)

The four hike-in camps in the park present a golden opportunity to the novice backpacker or the family that wants to spend a weekend outdoors without driving far. There is no fee for parking or camping, but *campers must register at the Visitor Center and get a permit.* Campsites may be reserved as long as two months in advance (phone 9 A.M.–noon weekdays, 663-1092), and if you hope to use one during a holiday weekend, you had better reserve it at least a month ahead of time.

All the camps contain toilets, tables, grills, hitch-rails, and water that is usually potable (but check with the Visitor Center during periods of drought). Wood fires are not allowed; use charcoal in the grills or a backpacking stove.

Because the peninsula is subject to frequent and unpredictable fogs, it's wise to take along some kind of cover for the night—if not a tent, at least a tarp.

The camps and some of the trails leading to them are described in subsequent pages. Incidentally, you don't have to backpack to visit these camps: each is close enough to some trailhead so that you can make it the destination for a picnic lunch on a one-day hike.

## Lodging

During the past decade, bed-and-breakfastry seems to have become the leading growth industry in West Marin. To find out about these places, many of which are located off the beaten track, you can phone one of the following services:

| | |
|---|---|
| Bed and Breakfast Cottages of Point Reyes | 663-9445 |
| Coastal Lodging | 485-2678 |
| Inns of Marin | 663-2000 |
| Inns of Point Reyes | 663-1420 |
| Point Reyes Lodging | 663-1872 |
| West Marin Chamber of Commerce | 663-9232 |
| West Marin Network | 663-9543 |

### Hostel

Laguna Ranch Hostel near Limantour Road is operated by the Golden Gate Council of American Youth Hostels, Inc. It is open every day of the year; check-in time is 4:30–9:30 P.M. Customs follow those of the international Youth Hostel As-

*Laguna Ranch Hostel is open every day*

*Paul Backhurst*

sociation: no pets, no alcohol, no smoking indoors; curfew at 11 P.M. Reservations are advised for groups larger than five. Office hours for reservations: 7:30–9:30 A.M. and 4:30–9:30 P.M.

> Laguna Ranch Hostel, Box 247
> Point Reyes Station, CA 94956
> Phone: 663-8811

The youth hostel occupies one of the buildings of the former Laguna Ranch. During World War II the US Army leased the ranch and installed barracks and gun emplacements. After the war Robert D. Marshall bought the ranch and ran cattle on it. He also planted a daffodil farm near the ranch house. Even though the NPS has owned the property since 1971, the remains of the daffodils continue to bloom here every spring, surprising and delighting hikers who happen upon them.

During the Vision Fire the firefighters managed to save the hostel by building a firebreak around it—but it was a near thing.

## Swimming

The best swimming in the area is at Tomales Bay State Park (see pp. 81–85).

It is possible to swim at Drakes and Limantour beaches, though neither has lifeguard service—and the water at both is cold. Drakes has a bathhouse.

The powerful surf and unpredictable undertow make the ocean beaches much too dangerous for wading or swimming.

*Swimmers and waders enjoy the warm water at Tomales Bay State Park*

## Bicycles

You can rent bikes at Trail Head Rentals (663-1958) at the corner of Highway 1 and Bear Valley Road—near the GGT #65 bus stop. The Bear Valley Visitor Center issues a free map showing bike routes within the park. See also "Regulations" below.

## Horses

Five Brooks Stables, located at the Five Brooks trailhead, offers guided trail rides, hay rides, and buggy rides in the National Seashore (9001 Highway 1, Olema, CA 94950; phone 663-1570). Equestrians are allowed on many of the park trails; for information, phone 663-1092.

## Llamas

Camelid Capers offers guided day trips in the Seashore with llamas as pack animals (Box 330, Inverness, CA 94937; phone 669-1523).

## Kayaks

Tamal Saka Tomales Bay Kayaking offers rentals, classes, and guided tours from the east side of Tomales Bay (Box 833, Marshall, CA 94940-0833; phone 663-1743).

Blue Waters Kayaking offers similar facilities on the west side of the bay, from the Golden Hinde Inn Marina in Inverness (phone 669-2600).

## Educational Programs

The rangers offer a variety of nature walks and other programs; inquire at the visitor centers.

The Point Reyes National Seashore Association in cooperation with the Seashore sponsors programs of the Point Reyes Field Seminar, for some of which Dominican College offers credit. They cover a wide variety of subjects in natural history, education, and the arts. Phone 663-1200, 10 A.M.–4 P.M. weekdays.

The following organizations conduct hikes and field trips in the National Seashore:

Golden Gate Audubon Society
2530 San Pablo Avenue,
   Suite G
Berkeley, CA 94702
Phone: (510) 843-2222

*Backpackers at Wildcat Camp hang their packs away from raccoons*

Marin Audubon Society
Box 599
Mill Valley, CA 94942-0599

Point Reyes National Sea-
   shore Association
Point Reyes Station, CA
   94956
Phone: (415) 663-1155

Sierra Club, San Francisco
   Bay Chapter
2530 San Pablo Avenue, #1
Berkeley, CA 94702
Phone: (510) 848-0800

## Education Center

The new Clem Miller Environmental Education Center opened early in 1987, replacing the former one, which had been based in a World War II Quonset hut. (The center is named for the Marin congressman who was killed in an airplane accident in 1962, shortly after he had steered through Congress the legislation establishing the National Seashore.) The new center, which took more than two years and almost a half million dollars to plan and construct, was financed through private donations, including those of the William Field Charitable Fund and the Buck Trust.

As with the hostel, the dedicated firefighters managed to save the center by surrounding it with a firebreak; only one outbuilding was burned.

# Regulations

The best way to keep up with park regulations is to pick up a copy of the free newsletter available at any of the visitor centers. Check out the section "What You Need to Know."

## Dogs

Proposals for governing dogs in the park have produced more intense and emotional testimony at Advisory Commission meetings than almost any other subject except transportation. In the same way that many automobile owners feel, "I want to drive, but everyone else should take the bus," many dog owners feel, "*My* dog is well trained and always under control, so it should be allowed to go to the park with me, even if other people's dogs misbehave." The facts remain, however, that most dogs if allowed to run free just naturally chase deer and other wildlife, and some of them harass equestrians, hikers, and bicyclists. And anyone who has hiked very long in the Bay Area knows that many dog owners simply ignore leash regulations. Therefore the National Seashore has adopted the following rules:

- No dogs are allowed on trails, in campgrounds, or on Drakes Beach, Abbotts Lagoon, McClures Beach, or Limantour Beach north of the parking lot.
- Dogs *on a leash no longer than 6 feet* are allowed on the following beaches: Kehoe, Point Reyes North and South, Palomarin, and Limantour south of the parking lot.

Headquarters issues a free list of dog rules for the Seashore and nearby parks.

## Bicycles

In the fall of 1984, NPS headquarters in Washington ruled that a clause in the 1964 Federal Wilderness Act barring all forms of "mechanical transport" in the wilderness areas applied to bicycles. This ruling may have resulted from the advent and immediate popularity of mountain bikes capable of running over rough terrain. In any event, it led to some highly charged meetings of the Advisory Commission for the GGNRA and Point Reyes. Bicycle enthusiasts pointed out that the 32,000 acres of the National Seashore designated as the Phillip Burton Wilderness include some of the trails that have traditionally been most popular with bicyclists, such as the southern ¾ mile of the Bear Valley Trail. The ruling still stands, however.

The visitor centers issue free maps showing permissible bike routes.

The NPS has posted the *following rules for bicycles*:

- Travel no faster than 15 miles per hour and slow down around blind curves. Bicyclists yield to both hikers and horses.
- Alert trail users ahead of you to your approach.
- Bicycles are not allowed off-trail or in designated wilderness areas, nor can they be walked or carried while on pedestrian trails.
- Bicycles are not allowed on the Earthquake Trail, the Woodpecker Trail, or at Kule Loklo.

## Camping

The campgrounds are described above under "Facilities." Remember that you must pick up a camping permit from the Bear Valley Visitor Center before starting out. Reservations may be made up to eight weeks ahead by calling 663-1092, 9 A.M.–noon, Monday through Friday.

Store food securely away from animals in the food storage lockers. Dispose of scraps in waste containers or carry out. Wash dishes away from water spigots.

Wood fires are not allowed at the campsites (see below, "Fires"). Use charcoal in the grills or use a backpacking stove to cook.

Quiet time is after sunset.

Stay within the designated site. Camping out of bounds is illegal.

## Fires

As a result of the disastrous Vision Fire, the park has implemented stricter rules about fires in the park. Specifically, *permits are now required for any wood fire ignited within the National Seashore*. Permits are available *free* from visitor centers, dispatch office, and field personnel.

Wood fires are allowed only on beaches, well away from any vegetation. They are allowed nowhere else. Wood must be brought in from outside the park, or reasonable amounts of driftwood can be gathered from beaches. The fire cannot be more than 36 inches in diameter.

Before leaving your beach fire, put it out completely with water. Do not cover coals up with sand as it will only insulate the heat and be an unseen danger to wildlife and barefoot visitors.

Charcoal fires are allowed in the Bear Valley and Drakes Beach picnic areas and the backcountry campgrounds in the grills provided. Visitors may also have charcoal fires in their own container or grill on beaches away from vegetation. Pack out used charcoal.

On days of either high or extreme fire danger, permits already issued will become void and new permits will not be available. During extreme fire danger periods, charcoal fires in contained grills on beaches, in campgrounds, or in picnic areas will also be banned. Only the use of self-contained camp stoves will then be allowed.

For updated weather information, including the level of fire danger on any particular day, phone 663-1092 ext. 402.

## Other Regulations

- In order to preserve natural, cultural, and archeological resources within the National Seashore, no collecting of natural objects or cultural artifacts (such as plants, flowers, seeds, nuts, antlers, or arrowheads) is allowed by law.
- No fireworks, firearms, or weapons of any sort are permitted.
- Motorcycles are not permitted on trails.

For fishing regulations, see pp. 14–15.

# Safety

Although West Marin may seem like a peaceful, bucolic scene far from the ills of the metropolis, a glance at the "Sheriff's Calls" in the *Point Reyes Light* reveals that it is not entirely crime-free. In particular, nearly every issue records an incident of "car clouting"—the theft of wallets, cameras, jewelry, clothing, camping gear, and/or other valuables from cars parked along roadsides or even in busy lots.

*Always leave cars locked with windows securely closed*, and never leave valuable objects visible within. Better yet, leave valuable objects at home.

The NPS advises the following for hikers:

- Stay on trails to avoid poison oak, stinging nettles, and ticks. Do not shortcut switchbacks; this causes erosion and damages trails.
- Wear layered clothing and be prepared for wind, rain, fog, and sunshine.
- Carry water and some food for longer hikes. Do not drink from streams: the protozoan *Giardia lamblia* may be present and can cause severe illness. Drinking water is available only at visitor centers and campgrounds.
- If horses need to pass you on the trail, step to the downhill side, greet the rider, and do not touch the animals.
- Observe warning signs on cliffs and beaches. It might seem unnecessary to belabor this point, yet people continue to get drowned along the coast because they ignore prominent signs warning of danger. *The most hazardous activities are*:
  - Climbing on the cliffs above the ocean.
  - Getting trapped on a pocket beach by incoming tide. If you plan to beachcomb, check the tide tables in advance. They are available at the Bear Valley Visitor Center.
  - Wading or swimming in the treacherous surf of the ocean beaches (North and South, Abbotts, Kehoe, and McClures): Severe rip currents exist, especially at North and South, and they can knock you down without notice. They can also carry off an unleashed dog.

For information about possibly dangerous animals, see above sections on mountain lions, ticks, and sharks.

# Maps

The visitor centers issue excellent free maps with useful and historical information, plus some showing bike routes, trail closures, and the like. Other maps available for sale at the Bear Valley Visitor Center and map stores in the Bay Area:

- Harrison, Tom, *Trail Map of Point Reyes National Seashore and Vicinity.* San Rafael: Tom Harrison Cartography, 1995. The most up-to-date map of the Seashore.
- Molenaar, Dee, *Pictorial Landform Map: Point Reyes National Seashore and the San Andreas Fault.* Rev. ed., Berkeley: Wilderness Press, 1993. Contains information about trails and facilities.
- *Erickson's Map of Point Reyes National Seashore and Tomales Bay & Taylor State Parks.*

The US Geological Survey issues the most detailed and authoritative maps. They are available at map stores and the USGS Western Regional Headquarters at 345 Middlefield Road, Menlo Park. "Point Reyes National Seashore and Vicinity" (scale 1:48,000) covers the whole peninsula and much of West Marin. The five 7.5-minute topographic maps (scale 1:24,000) covering the National Seashore are: Tomales, Drakes Bay, Inverness, Double Point, and Bolinas.

Many of the trails in the Seashore are old ranch roads that the Park Service has designated as official trails by mapping and signing them. There are a great many more old roads and trails that are not signed or officially maintained and that are not on any of the maps. Energetic and intrepid hikers can explore these at their leisure. If you know how to use a compass and the topographic maps, you will probably not get lost. A greater danger is poison oak, which abounds on some of the unmaintained trails.

# Nearby Towns

### Olema *(probably Coast Miwok for* coyote*)*

This town at the crossroads of Drake Highway and Highway 1 was once the metropolis of West Marin. In the early 1870s it featured two hotels, six (!) bars, and biweekly stagecoach service to San Rafael. When the North Pacific Coast Railroad was built in 1875, it bypassed Olema in favor of Point Reyes Station, which subsequently became the metropolis of West Marin.

Olema is the nearest town to the main entrance to the National Seashore. It now contains two delis and two restaurants—the Farm House and the Olema Inn. The Inn, built in 1876, has been lovingly restored and now operates also as a bed-and-breakfast lodging. There are several other b&bs in or near town, including the ornate Point Reyes Seashore Lodge north of the Farm House.

Just north of downtown on Highway 1 is the Olema Ranch Campground (on what was once an artichoke field). The campground offers sites for tents and RVs and contains a laundromat and a gas station—one of the few remaining on the Marin coast. Phone: 663-8001 or 800-655-CAMP.

When country singer Merle Haggard recorded "Okie from Muskogee," rock star Jesse Colin Young took offense at Haggard's redneck lyrics and countered with a record called "Hippie from Olema."

*Coastal Traveler*, Winter 1987

## Point Reyes Station

From 1875 until 1933 this town was centered on the North Pacific Coast Railroad, and some of the evidence remains: the former depot is now the post office, and the former engine house is now a community center, the Red Barn. Since the departure of the trains, the main industry supporting the town has been dairy farming. In testimony to its importance is the fact that the town has, instead of a noon whistle, a noon moo.

At present Point Reyes Station is an intriguing mixture of the agricultural and the touristic. In addition to businesses providing supplies to ranchers and ranch hands, it contains two bars, a few restaurants (one of them the elegant Station House Cafe), a large market, a bakery, two bookstores, and an assortment of art galleries and antique stores. Also—useful for visitors to know—a gas station and a bank with an ATM machine. The Dance Palace (503 B Street), a community center built mainly by volunteers, is one of the leading purveyors of culture in West Marin—everything from local choral groups to jazz musicians from San Francisco. If you're spending a weekend in the area and want to know what's going on, call 663-1075, or check the "Announcements" section in the *Point Reyes Light* classifieds.

Point Reyes Station still retains enough of its small-Western-town appearance that director John Carpenter used it as the setting for the movie *Village of the Damned*, shot in the town and its environs in 1994. I have not seen this film, but I gather from the reviews that it will probably not win many Oscars, except perhaps for its photography of the magnificent West Marin scenery.

In 1995 the Walt Disney Studios wanted to use Point Reyes Station as the location for *Phenomenon*, starring John Travolta. Much to the megacorporation's astonishment, the Village Association turned them down. The local businesspeople and other citizens felt that closing Main Street for 10 straight business days would cause more disruption than the reported $10,000 the studio was willing to recompense them was worth.

Perhaps the town's greatest claim to fame is its weekly, the *Point Reyes Light*, edited by David V. Mitchell. In 1979 the *Light* won the Pulitzer Prize—rarely accorded a weekly—for its investigatory reporting on neighboring Synanon Foundation (see below, "MARCONI"). Aficionados of offbeat journalism relish the deadpan "Sheriff's Calls" that appear in each issue and illuminate life in West Marin. For example:

- **Point Reyes Station**—A resident reported a suspicious person trespassing on his property. The man was described as wearing nose rings with beads and feathers and carrying the leg of a deer in his belt. He also wore a necklace of small animal skulls and rode a bicycle with antlers mounted on the handlebars.
- **Inverness Park**—An ornithologist reported a fresh grave at the Shield's Nature Preserve. After digging for 30 minutes, a deputy unearthed a box

containing a dead cat, which he reburied.

- **Bolinas**—A citizen reported spotting a dead calf in front of a ranch. When the rancher checked, he found a human body instead of a calf but could not determine whether it was still breathing. He notified deputies but later called back to say the body had gotten up and staggered away.
- **Lucas Valley Road**—A motorist notified deputies that she had seen a body lying face-down in a ditch. An officer checked and found a photographer taking pictures of flowers.
- **Nicasio**—A man declaring himself to be the second coming of Christ showed up at a business. Deputies arrested him on warrants issued in Palo Alto.

## Inverness Park

This is basically a wide spot on Sir Francis Drake Highway about 1¼ mile west of Highway 1. It contains a grocery store-with-deli and a bakery-with-coffee shop. Tucked away in the woods are some b&bs and a crafts shop.

It was in the upper reaches of Inverness Park, in the Paradise Ranch Estates section, that many homes were destroyed in the Vision Fire. The roads leading up the ridge are winding and narrow—difficult for fire trucks to negotiate—and many of the greenery-loving residents had surrounded their houses closely with trees and shrubbery. For a back view of this area, try the Inverness Ridge Trail.

## Inverness

When you drive to the western beaches of the National Seashore, you will pass through Inverness, founded as a resort town in the hope of restoring the Shafter family fortunes (see p. 17). The Shafter forebears were Scottish; hence the name of the town and streets such as Argyle and Cameron. Inverness contains several restaurants, including the venerable Vladimir's (Czech) and Manka's Inverness Lodge (formerly Czech, but now more ecumenical and emphasizing wild game). The town also has a grocery store-with-deli, a garage and gas station, and innumerable b&bs.

About a block up Inverness Way from Sir Francis Drake, at 15 Park Way, is the Inverness Library and Jack Mason Museum of West Marin History. Jack Mason, who devoted the latter part of his life to writing and publishing books about West Marin history—and whom I have quoted frequently throughout this book—died in January 1985. Shortly before his death he willed his house, The Gables, to the Inverness Foundation to function as a museum for his collection of West Marin memorabilia and to house the Inverness public library, which for years operated out of a funky one-room building no larger than a bookmobile. It was, in fact, the smallest free-standing library in the nation! (The building, just north of the garage, now houses a real-estate office.)

With the enthusiastic support of the community—and a grant from the Buck Fund —Mason's Victorian home has been turned into a charming structure housing an enlarged library and a museum containing his invaluable collection of photos, books, manuscripts, and artifacts connected with Marin history.

Hours: 3–6 P.M. and 7–9 P.M. Monday; 10 A.M.–1 P.M. and 2–6 P.M. Tuesday and

Wednesday; 3–6 P.M. Friday; 10 A.M.–1 P.M. Saturday. The museum alone is some-times open on Sunday afternoon. Phone: 669-1288 (library), 669-1066 (museum).

## Bolinas

Bolinas has now achieved world-wide fame as the town that wants no one to know where it is. For 20 years Caltrans put up signs on Highway 1 indicating the turnoff to Bolinas, and every one was soon torn down at night by the informal Bolinas Border Patrol. John Grissim noted in the *Point Reyes Light* of October 27, 1988, ". . . no less than 34 Bolinas road signs have been spirited away since 1974 (some of which adorn living rooms in Paris and Katmandu . . .").

In November 1989 Caltrans, claiming that the silent majority of townspeople really wanted the sign and only a few malcontents were tearing it down, con-ducted an advisory poll. The result: 73 percent of the voters rejected the sign. At that point Caltrans gave up.

Bolinas's attempts to deter visitors are due not solely to xenophobia (although a few inhabitants have on occasion pelted chartered tourist buses with eggs) but also to the town's layout: the main entrance road splits downtown into two branches, each of which deadends after about two blocks. Hence any major tour-ist traffic soon creates gridlock.

The fact remains that to get to the Palomarin trailhead of the National Sea-shore, you have to skirt Bolinas. And you may want to visit the town itself, which has restaurants, a historic bar (Smiley's), a grocery store, and a gas station—some-thing that nearby Stinson Beach currently lacks. The town isn't that hard to find: just take the first road heading toward the ocean from north of Bolinas Lagoon.

### Recommended reading:

Arrigoni, Patricia, *Making the Most of Marin*. Rev. ed., Fairfax, CA: Travel Publish-ers International, 1990.

Teather, Louise, *Place Names of Marin: Where Did They Come From?* San Francisco: Scottwall Associates, 1986.

## *Where to go for more information:*

The *Point Reyes Light* issues a free quarterly publication called *Coastal Traveler* which can be found at most businesses in West Marin. It gives up-to-date infor-mation on restaurants, lodgings, stores, etc. from Marin north to Mendocino and Lake counties.

The back page of each issue of the weekly *Point Reyes Light* contains a "Visitor's Guide to the Coast."

When driving near Bear Valley headquarters or the lighthouse, turn to 1610 on the AM radio for an update on what's happening in the Seashore.

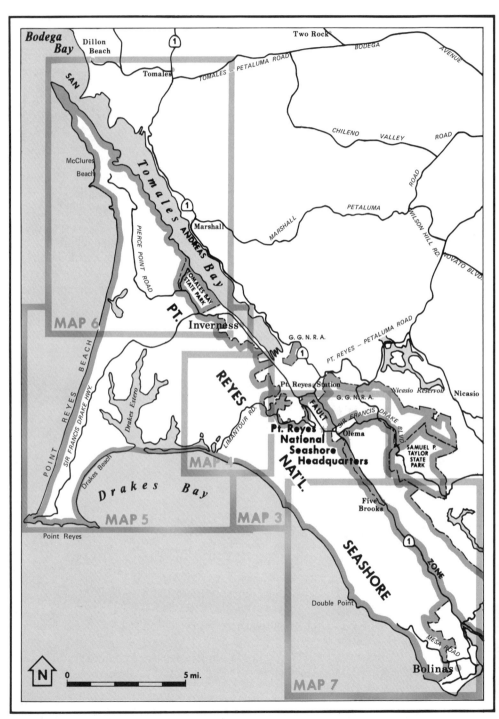

**TOWNS NEAR THE NATIONAL SEASHORE**
**MAP 2**

LEGEND: ———— Roads
············ Trail
▬▬▬·· Park Bdy.
✪ Campground

# The Trails

# Bear Valley and Glen Camp

## National Seashore Headquarters

The Red Barn on the left side of the access road to the park formerly housed the Visitor Center. The *W* still visible on its cupola indicates that it was part of Charles Webb Howard's showplace W Ranch. It was not really suitable for a visitor center, because it straddles the San Andreas Fault (!) and in fact was damaged in the 1906 quake.

The present Bear Valley Visitor Center opened in November 1983. It was financed with $1.4 million in private grants from the William Field Fund and the Buck Fund (via the San Francisco Foundation). The architects—Bull, Field, Volkmann, Stockwell—designed a 7,600-square-foot barnlike structure intended to fit well into the surrounding pastoral landscape. It contains an auditorium, a library, office space, and an extensive and fascinating exhibit area, created by Daniel Quan Design.

*The Visitor Center—your first stop*

Paul Backhurst

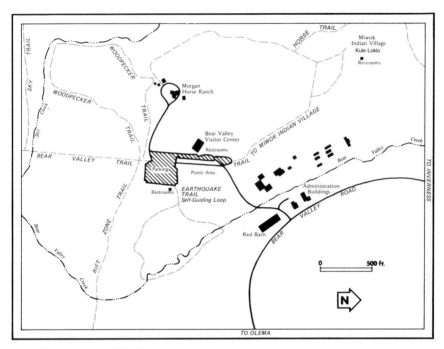

**BEAR VALLEY HEADQUARTERS AREA**
## MAP 2a

The *San Francisco Chronicle*'s Pulitzer Prize-winning architectural critic, Alan Temko, wrote (October 5, 1987):

> Architecturally and educationally, it is surely one of the best of its kind built recently in the national park system. There is a consideration for the individual, a kindness really, that is inseparable from the respect shown to the building's surroundings.

The Visitor Center should be your first stop in the park. Here you can pick up free maps and information sheets, find out what nature programs and other activities are scheduled, and browse in the book store. (Visitor Center open 9 A.M.– 5 P.M. weekdays, 8 A.M.–5 P.M. weekends and holidays; phone 663-1092; water, restrooms, phone. All facilities are wheelchair accessible, and a wheelchair is available for borrowing.)

First-time visitors to the park, tourists with little time to spare, and families with small children may wish to spend their entire stay in the Bear Valley area, rambling the short trails described below. Eventually the Park Service may establish a food concession here, but at present visitors must bring food or pick it up at one of the nearby communities if they wish to picnic at tables on the pleasant grounds under majestic firs, oaks, and bay trees.

The Bear Valley area was not damaged by the Vision Fire of October 1995 because the firefighters succeeded in establishing its perimeter on Sky Trail, up-hill to the northwest. The Bear Valley Visitor Center, however, became the central command post for firefighting activity, and the area was closed to the public for several days.

## The Earthquake Trail

This is a paved, 0.6-mile self-guiding nature trail that is completely wheel-chair accessible. Those on foot will appreciate this gentle trail also, as it winds across Bear Valley Creek under willows and oak trees in the area along the San Andreas Fault Zone where the land shifted abruptly by as much as 20 feet during the big quake of 1906.

Plaques along the route illustrate plate tectonics, the damage of 1906, and other quake-related information. (As noted above in "Geology" the 1989 Loma Prieta quake had very little effect here.) Rangers conduct guided programs along the trail on weekends; consult the schedule at the Visitor Center.

More ambitious hikers who are seeking the Rift Zone Trail (see p. 47) can look for the trailhead sign just south of the Bear Valley parking lot.

## Kule Loklo, the Miwok Village

You can gain some idea of how the original inhabitants of Point Reyes lived by paying a visit to the village of Kule Loklo (the Coast Miwok words for Bear Valley) less than a half mile north of headquarters. The village started in 1976 as a cooperative Bicentennial venture among the National Park Service, the Miwok Archeological Preserve of Marin, and a local school district. Much of the work has been done by schoolchildren and volunteers.

In the spring of 1992 an arsonist torched Kule Loklo's ceremonial dance house. The Coast Miwok elders selected a new site for rebuilding the structure, and work began. Once again thousands of hours were donated by volunteers, including park employees and Native Americans from several tribes. The dance house is now restored, and Kule Loklo is the site of occasional Miwok festivals. Rangers and volunteers also conduct regular cultural demonstrations; check schedules at the Bear Valley Visitor Center. This is an excellent place to take children.

## Woodpecker Trail and the Morgan Horse Ranch

The 0.7-mile Woodpecker Trail begins just north of the Bear Valley parking lot and trailhead, on the right, then runs gently uphill toward the forest. The self-guiding trail is marked by explanatory posts that point out the main kinds of trees and other natural features of the Point Reyes area, including a particular Douglas fir which has been much favored by California woodpeckers.

Still in the forest, the trail curves north and east around a small meadow. If you are lucky and quiet, you may see some white fallow deer browsing here. Now the trail nears a red barn/museum where you can study the fascinating history of the Morgan horse, the first truly American breed. All Morgans are descended from one superequine, a stallion who died in 1821 after distinguishing himself for strength, speed, and endurance. After studying their background, you can watch the park's current herd of Morgans frisking about in their corral. The

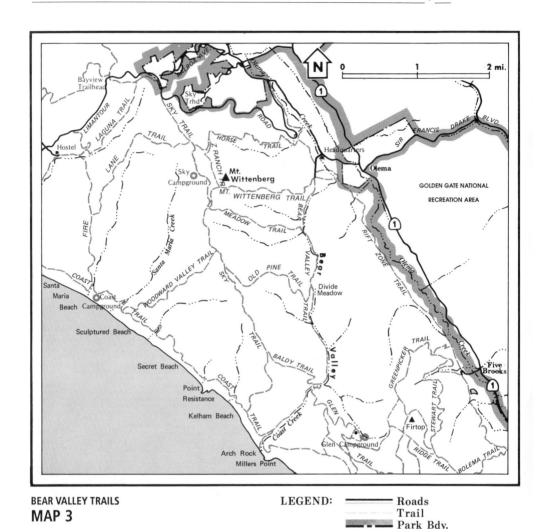

**BEAR VALLEY TRAILS**
**MAP 3**

LEGEND: ———— Roads
⋯⋯⋯ Trail
▬▬▬ Park Bdy.
○ Campground

Park Service raises these horses to provide visitors—especially city children—a chance to experience first hand an important part of our country's heritage, and also to provide mounts for rangers at the Seashore and other national parks.

## Bear Valley Trail

*Facilities:* There is no drinking water anywhere along the route. There are toilets and picnic tables at Divide Meadow, roughly the midpoint. If you hope to go to the beach at the end of the trail, you should pick up a tide table at the Visitor Center.

*Regulations:* No horses are permitted on weekends or holidays. The final ¾ mile is in the Phillip Burton Wilderness Area, and therefore off limits to bikes.

This is undoubtedly the most popular trail in the National Seashore—and with good reason. It's an easy, fairly level 4.4-mile walk beside murmuring streams, under towering trees, and through a broad, peaceful meadow, eventually arriving at the sea. Don't expect solitude, however: this trail is generally thronged with hikers on weekends.

The trailhead is just south of the parking lot. It was in this area that Gene Compton, who had bought the Bear Valley Ranch in 1943, staged annual rodeos from 1946 to 1948. As you start out on the trail you will be walking beside Bear Valley Creek. This stream runs north— the opposite direction from the stream you will hike along after passing the meadow. Odd drainage patterns are characteristic of the fault zone. The Bear Valley Trail is also extremely susceptible to storm damage. Much of the trail had to be rebuilt after the storm of January 1982 and again after the storms of spring 1995.

In ¼ mile you pass the junction with the Mt. Wittenberg Trail (formerly a section of the Sky Trail, but rechristened in 1995), marked by a gigantic bay tree with many trunks. Now you enter a forested area, with bay, Douglas fir, bishop pine, buckeye, hazel, elderberry, and, along the stream, alder. (On your left, across the creek, a venerable dogwood tree is visible when it blossoms in the spring.)

In places the larger trees arch over the trail to form a leafy tunnel through which sunlight filters. Ferns abound on the mossy banks—five-finger and maidenhair, as well as the more common sword and bracken ferns. If you are hiking in spring, you will find buttercup, iris, miner's lettuce, bleeding heart, wild cucumber, blue forget-me-not, English daisy, and—if you look closely along the stream bank—wild ginger.

**Rest stop at Divide Meadow on the Bear Valley Trail**

After 1.6 miles of gentle ascent from the trailhead, you arrive at Divide Meadow (toilets, picnic tables). San Francisco's elite Pacific Union Club maintained its hunting lodge here from the 1890s until the Great Depression. Their quarry included bear and mountain lion, as well as deer.

Helen Bingham, who visited Point Reyes in 1906, described Bear Valley in her book *In Tamal Land:*

> One can drive through its cool depths on a finely graded road amid thousands of majestic trees, while here and there an open space reveals the sunlight and the blue sky overhead in contrast with the dim uncertain light pervading its woodland stretches.

She took a dim view of the hunt club, however:

> The deep baying of hounds from its extensive kennels forms the only discordant note in the Valley, reminding one that even near to nature's heart man's inherent primitiveness asserts itself. If, when wandering in these woodland fastnesses, he (man) would hunt the wild creatures with a camera it

would require greater patience, skill and acumen than making the ground wet with the blood of fawns and quail.

As we walk through the now-peaceful meadow, it is pleasant to observe that Miss Bingham's wish has been fulfilled.

After following the edge of the long meadow, the trail reenters forest. The stream accompanying it now is Coast Creek, which flows into the ocean. The unusually large buckeyes along this part of the trail are magnificent in late spring, when their candles of pinkish-cream flowers are blooming. At 3.2 miles, where the trail to Glen Camp takes off to the left, bicyclists must dismount and continue on foot.

*Returning toward the Bear Valley trailhead under arching bay trees*

Finally you come out on a meadow about 50 feet above the sea—an old marine terrace that has been raised sometime within the last 100,000 years. If the tide is low enough, you can descend a steep trail to the beach and a natural rock tunnel through which the creek flows. Or you can walk out Millers Point to look up and down the coast. The point is named for Clem Miller, the Congressman who was so influential in establishing the National Seashore, and whose gravesite is located a few hundred feet south, uphill, off the Coast Trail. His resting place was donated to the park by rancher Bruce Kelham, who owned Bear Valley Ranch from 1949 to 1963: this half-acre was the first property to be acquired by the National Seashore.

Some friends of mine who have been hiking the Bear Valley Trail with their family regularly for many years, comment:

> Millers Point is a spectacular place for a picnic, if the sky is clear and the wind not too strong; all of Drakes Bay, from Chimney Rock to Double Point, will be in view—and on a *very* clear day the Farallons as well. (However, the cliffs are dangerous: this is not a place for unattended small children!)

You can return to the trailhead the way you came, or if your day is still young and you don't mind a climb, you can use your trail map to work out an alternative route or a scenic detour. The family quoted above notes:

> Our favorite (if the tide is not too high) is to go through the tunnel to the beach, and up Kelham Beach to the right all the way to Point Resistance,

where there is a great cavern to explore. (However, anyone doing this must keep a close eye on the tide: there are several points that become impassable at high tide.)

## Rift Zone Trail

*How to get there:* The trail runs for about 4½ level miles between Bear Valley and Five Brooks.

- *By bus:* If you come by bus, you necessarily start at Bear Valley and either walk round-trip, or make a long loop by way of Firtop and/or Glen Camp, or cadge a ride back from the Five Brooks parking lot to the Bear Valley bus stop.
- *By car:* You can park at either Bear Valley or Five Brooks, 3½ car miles south. If you want to walk the trail just one way, you can arrange a car shuttle, leaving one car in each parking lot. Since the route is virtually level, it doesn't much matter which direction you choose to walk in. I have arbitrarily written it up as starting from Bear Valley because that's where the bus stops.

*Facilities:* Water, restrooms, and picnic tables at Five Brooks; all these plus phone and other amenities at Bear Valley.

*Regulations:* The trail crosses land belonging to the Vedanta Society, and hikers should observe their rules: open 8 A.M. until two hours before sunset; no wheeled vehicles, no hunting, no dogs or other pets, no fires or smoking, no camping or picnicking. There are many livestock gates along the route, which hikers should close after going through them.

The first time I tried this trail was at the end of a long, dry summer. Not only was the trail extremely dusty to begin with, but as we hiked north from Five Brooks we encountered over a hundred equestrians spread out along it, who—although friendly—could hardly avoid stirring up even more dust. I mentally wrote this trail off as suitable mainly for horsepersons, and repaired to the Farm House in Olema for a beer.

A year and a half later, some visitors from the East Coast expressed such eagerness to hike along the San Andreas Fault Zone that I agreed to accompany them from Bear Valley to Five Brooks. It was a warm day in early April, and the countryside still sported the vivid early-Technicolor green that exhilarates inhabitants of northern California for about three weeks of every year. Over the entire 4½ miles we encountered only three other hikers and one equestrian. The Easterners were so entranced by the idyllic gorgeousness of this trail that they begged me never to publicize it. (But duty prevails.) Note that the pasture areas of the trail can get muddy during the wet season.

The Rift Zone Trail begins just south of the Bear Valley parking lot, where a sign indicates FIVE BROOKS. The trail runs across a flat, tundralike expanse, then past some giant bay trees. It crosses Bear Valley Creek and ascends a knoll under bay trees and coast live oaks. You go through a self-closing livestock gate and traverse a meadow, heading toward the line of eucalyptus and Monterey cypress that marks the road to the Vedanta Society Retreat. Two gates permit hikers to cross this road. In the next 3 miles you will be hiking on Vedanta Society land.

The Vedanta Society is a religious organization whose beliefs are basically East Indian in origin. Its main northern California headquarters is at 2323 Vallejo Street, San Francisco 94123 (phone 922-2323). Its Olema Retreat is designed to "provide opportunity to spiritual seekers of all faiths to meditate and study in a secluded area of meadows and forests away from the disturbances of urban life." Originally this land belonged to Judge James

*From the Rift Zone Trail hikers can get a glimpse of the Vedanta Society Retreat*

McMillan Shafter and after him his son Payne. The Vedanta Society purchased it in 1946. According to a long-standing agreement with the Department of the Interior, the society may continue to maintain its 2000-plus acres as a religious retreat, with the stipulation that if it ever desires to sell any of its land the National Seashore will have the first option to buy it.

Once past the Vedanta Society's gate you make your way across a large field, heading southeast. Soon the old Shafter mansion, "The Oaks," comes into view. In 1875 Judge Shafter gave this magnificent house, built in 1869, along with 2235 surrounding acres, to his son Payne as a 30th birthday present. (He made no such gift to his daughter Julia, who as her father's executrix had to spend much of her life doggedly trying to pay off his debts.) The house is now headquarters for the Vedanta Society Retreat. A number of devotees live here permanently and raise fruit and vegetables; hence the barn and other outbuildings. From time to time they offer an open house to the general public.

Now the Rift Zone Trail heads south across the field. The trail may be a bit hard to discern when the grass is tall, but it is marked by occasional posts. Eventually you arrive at a corral, and perhaps some Black Angus cattle. Going counterclockwise around the corral and through another gate, you turn left on an old farm road.

The next 2 miles are on this road, which runs south through countryside of great beauty and variety. Cool ferny forests alternate with tranquil meadows and mysterious marshes. Occasional fallen bay trees form leafy arches over the trail. You are paralleling Highway 1 (as well as Olema Creek and the San Andreas Fault Zone) but are just far enough away from it not to hear auto noises.

Shortly after leaving Vedanta property you switchback down, ford a creek and pass a trail that leads to Firtop. Just beyond this junction bear right, uphill, to continue on the Rift Zone Trail. After passing another marsh and fording another creek you arrive at a horse camp (picnic tables). Walk across its clearing heading south toward a cottage that has undergone several metamorphoses in recent years, including a New England phase and a Russian one; at this writing it is undergoing yet another transformation. You go briefly back into forest and soon emerge on the main road headed for the Five Brooks parking lot. Along the way you get a good view of Bolinas Ridge to the east.

## Glen Camp

*Facilities:* Water, but during some seasons it is not potable—find out from headquarters in advance; toilets, picnic tables, grills, hitchrail.

*Regulations:* No dogs, no open fires. (It is not a regulation, but insect repellent is advisable in warm weather.)

In some respects Glen Camp is the most attractive of the backpacking camps in the National Seashore. True, it lacks the views one gets at Sky Camp, and it lacks the beaches one finds at Wildcat and Coast camps. But its campsites are more widely dispersed, and some are sheltered under towering trees, so that a camper gets a little more feeling of remoteness.

Like all the campgrounds in the National Seashore, Glen is located on what was once the site of a ranch—Glen Ranch, part of the J.M. Shafter empire. It was abandoned in the 1920s and none of its buildings remain.

A glance at the map reveals that Glen Camp can be approached from either Bear Valley trailhead or Five Brooks trailhead. Although Five Brooks is closer to the camp as the crow flies, the route from Bear Valley is leveller. Take the Bear Valley Trail 3.2 miles to the clearly marked turnoff to Glen Trail on the left. (In spring, a purple nightshade blooms on your right just before the turnoff.) The Glen Trail (more of a fire road at this point) leads uphill and through a meadow. After ½ mile the Glen Camp Loop Trail branches left and becomes a tree-shaded path skirting a canyon. You walk through coffeeberry and lots of blackberry, and at one point cross a stream. Following the signs to Glen Camp, you make a short descent past a marshy pond and then a brief climb into the protected glade around which the campsites are scattered.

The quickest, easiest way to return is the way you came. However, if you've camped overnight, and lightened your pack by eating and drinking part of the contents, you may be up for a somewhat more ambitious hike. A look at the map

**The trail to Glen Campground passes under majestic old Douglas firs**

**Campsites are spread out around the glen; some are sheltered by trees**

reveals several possibilities. For example, you can go back to the Bear Valley Trail, cross it, and return to the trailhead via Baldy and Sky trails and Mt. Wittenberg (about 6 miles, including an elevation gain of over 1300 feet). Or you can take one of the trails to Five Brooks and then hike the 4½-mile Rift Zone Trail back to head-quarters—or hitchhike back with a hiker who has parked at Five Brooks.

Or you can wander over to the Coast Trail and take it back to Bear Valley. This route will take you through some of the wildest and least traveled areas of the park. Parts of the Coast Trail south of Bear Valley are steep, rocky and rugged. Clem Miller, the late Congressman who was probably more responsible than any other one person for establishing the National Seashore, is buried under a simple stone a short distance from the Coast Trail, on a bluff overlooking the ocean above the point that bears his name.

# Mt. Wittenberg and Sky Camp

*How to get there:* The shortest, levellest route to Sky Camp and Mt. Wittenberg is from the Sky Trailhead on the Limantour Road (see p. 61)—about a 4½-mile round trip if you climb the mountain. Novice or lazy backpackers may want to take this route to the camp (not forgetting to get a permit from the Bear Valley Visitor Center first).

Otherwise, begin at the Bear Valley trailhead.

*Facilities:* Water, toilets, picnic tables, grills, hitchrail at Sky Camp.

*Regulations:* No dogs, no open fires.

Mt. Wittenberg, at 1407 feet, is the highest point in the National Seashore and offers a grand view over the surrounding country. On its western flank is Sky Camp, one of four backpacking camps in the park, and the one closest to headquarters. Most of the original campsites at Sky were on an exposed glade and therefore somewhat lacking in privacy, but in recent years the Park Service has re-sited them to provide more-sheltered spaces. The camp was burned in the Vision Fire and was closed for several months, but in April 1996 it reopened and now is substantially back to normal except for burned trees and cut-down eucalyptus, which will resprout.

The camp is located on the site of C. W. Howard's Z Ranch. The mountain derived its name from two Wittenberg brothers who were tenants during the 1860s. Nothing remains of the ranch today except the burned and cut trees and the spring that now provides water to the camp. In 1995 the NPS christened a trail near the summit of Mt. Wittenberg the Z Ranch Trail.

Mt. Wittenberg is an excellent destination for a day hike, planning lunch for either the summit or Sky Camp. With the aid of your trail map, you can choose among several possible routes of varying degrees of steepness and devise a loop trip to suit your mood and the weather.

## Trails from Bear Valley to Sky Trail

As noted above, the firefighters of October 1995 finally established a southern perimeter by bulldozing the Sky Trail all the way down its length and dropping fire retardant on it from air tankers. Nature will eventually restore the trail, but perhaps with some different vegetation. The trails leading from Bear Valley to the Sky Trail—described in the following pages—were essentially undamaged.

## Mt. Wittenberg Trail

This trail used to be considered part of the Sky Trail, but in 1995 the NPS rechristened it. It is the most direct hiking route to Sky Camp (except for the route from the Sky Trailhead on the Limantour Road, mentioned above)—only 2½ miles—but it is also the steepest. Novice backpackers and leisurely picnickers may prefer one of the gentler routes.

Start on the Bear Valley Trail, and in ¼ mile turn right on the clearly marked Mt. Wittenberg Trail at the great multiple-trunked bay tree. The trail ascends under hazel, tanbark oak, and Douglas fir; a profusion of sword ferns carpets the ground. About halfway up the mountain you come to a near-level clearing somewhat larger than a football field where you can catch your breath. In fall you can search for huckleberries in the lush growth bordering the clearing.

The trail now continues up an open slope dotted with firs, then goes steeply through forest again and finally emerges on a hillside not far from the top of the mountain. A short trail leads to the summit. From here you have a 360-degree view of the entire Point Reyes peninsula and the esteros, Tomales Bay, Black Mountain (also known as Elephant Mountain) behind Point Reyes Station, the lush Olema Valley, and Bolinas Ridge; and in clear weather Mts. St. Helena, Diablo, and Tamalpais.

*Before the final ascent of Mt. Wittenberg, the trail levels off in a long meadow*

From the summit you descend south to rejoin the trail. Here you can turn right to reach Sky Camp, or turn left to take one of the trails leading back to Bear Valley or the coast.

## Meadow Trail

*Regulations:* No horses on weekends and holidays.

This route offers hikers and backpackers a more gradual ascent to Sky Camp than the Mt. Wittenberg Trail. Take the Bear Valley Trail past the Mt. Wittenberg Trail junction and turn right on the Meadow Trail, 0.8 mile from the trailhead. The trail crosses a footbridge and ascends through pungent bay, tall Douglas fir, dense sword fern, and bushy huckleberry. In fact, all the trails on the eastern slope of Wittenberg offer plenty of opportunities for huckleberrying in late summer and early fall.

On one cool November day on which I hiked here, the forest silence was broken only by the songs of a couple of varied thrushes. It was the first clear day after a week of rain, and I found an incredibly lush and varied growth of mushrooms (which I was, however, much too prudent to harvest).

The trail soon reaches the long meadow of its name. On that visit, I encountered in the very center of the long meadow a solitary young man in the half-lotus position playing a flute. Perhaps he was trying to charm some of the animals out of the ground. To judge from the number of burrows, the meadow must support a considerable subterranean population of rabbits, weasels, badgers, and foxes—

or, more likely, gophers. If there are no flute players, and you come by yourself or in a small, quiet group, you have an excellent chance of seeing deer.

From the meadow, the trail reenters forest and continues to ascend gently, occasionally overlooking a deep, wooded canyon. The trees here are so tall that as you walk beneath them you can hear the wind soughing in their tops, sounding like a distant waterfall, but you cannot feel it. Soon you reach the Sky Trail junction, and from here it's only a level half mile straight ahead to the camp. If the day is clear, you will have views of Limantour Spit and Drakes Bay as you contour along the slope of Mt. Wittenberg.

## Horse Trail

Hikers seldom use this trail, perhaps because they figure it's the province of horses; but if you try it on a weekday you probably won't run into many equestrians. It provides a different and pleasant way to reach Sky Camp. (It can, however, get muddy in places during the rainy season; and slogging through mud that has just been trodden by horses will test the mettle—and the boots—of even the most dedicated hiker.) It is an old ranch road.

From the Bear Valley parking lot, head toward Kule Loklo, the Miwok Village, to find the Horse Trail. After crossing a creek on a footbridge it ascends gradually under huge bay trees, then hazel, tanbark oak, and Douglas fir. After almost 2 miles of steady climb the trail comes out into the open in a mass of coyote brush. Soon you come to the Z Ranch Trail that leads to Mt. Wittenberg. If you continue on the Horse Trail, you contour along a steep, firry canyon for 0.4 mile, pass a meadow with lupine and rattlesnake grass, and arrive at a junction with the Sky Trail. From here it's only another 0.4 mile to the camp.

## Old Pine Trail

*Regulations:* No horses on weekends and holidays.

This is one of my favorite trails in the Seashore. It is, however, very susceptible to storm damage. I found this out the hard way one November day when I introduced a friend to it after a series of storms. We approached from the Bear Valley end and spent a couple of hours climbing over and under down trees. You might want to check with the Bear Valley Visitor Center about the condition of the trail if you plan to take it after a storm.

Assuming no storm damage, this is a beautiful trail in either direction and provides a relatively easy ascent from Divide Meadow to Sky Camp and Mt. Wittenberg.

On the Bear Valley Trail proceed 1.6 miles to Divide Meadow (toilets, picnic tables) and find the Old Pine Trail on the right. The trail gets its name from a small grove of bishop pines in the forest, but most of the trees you will be ascending under are majestic, moss-covered firs that reach straight above you for a hundred feet or more. Some have leather fern growing from their trunks and branches, and elderberry, huckleberry, and salal provide a green undergrowth. This dense forest conveys a sense of peace—and yet of mystery, too.

After 1.9 miles the Old Pine Trail meets the Sky Trail and shortly thereafter you arrive at a junction with the Woodward Valley Trail. You can take it 1.7 miles down to the coast; or you can continue on the Sky Trail to the camp; or you can make a loop back to Bear Valley via the Meadow Trail or the Mt. Wittenberg Trail.

# Trails from Sky Camp to the coast

## Sky Trail

As noted above, this trail was bulldozed to form the southern firebreak during the Vision Fire. While this book was in preparation, the lower part of the trail was still closed, but was scheduled to reopen soon. Like all the trails in the burn area, it offers hikers an unprecedented opportunity to watch nature restoring itself.

## Woodward Valley Trail

Before the Vision Fire, this was one of the most attractive trails in the Seashore—and no doubt it will be again. At least the views will remain, although the vegetation may be somewhat changed. The following description was written *pre-Fire*. Curious hikers may be interested in comparing it with what they see on this trail now.

> This varied trail alternates dense forest with open greensward, and features occasional sudden and spectacular views over Drakes Bay and the ocean. Because of the views and the occasional steep stretches, I prefer to hike this trail heading west—that is to say, descending.
>
> The Woodward Valley Trail branches off the Sky Trail 1.4 miles from Sky Camp at a glade. The trail enters forest, then passes through a long, enchanted meadow fringed with firs. It is tempting just to throw down one's daypack and spend the day here, snoozing and hoping for a visit from the white deer—or even a unicorn.
>
> From the meadow you continue back into the forest, then soon emerge into the open and a view of Limantour; if the weather is clear enough, the Farallon Islands are visible on the horizon 20 miles out to sea. From here on, the trail goes in and out of woods, generally descending—at times steeply. Soon the panorama includes the whole of Drakes Bay from Double Point to Point Reyes.
>
> At 1.7 miles from the Sky Trail junction, the Woodward Valley Trail joins the Coast Trail just above Sculptured Beach (see p. 56). You can visit the beach if the tide is low enough, and then proceed south to Bear Valley or north to Coast Camp and Limantour.

## Fire Lane Trail

The Fire Lane Trail, which begins about a half mile north of Sky Camp and runs for just over 3 miles to Coast Camp, mostly descending, is the most direct route. It is not as elegant as the variegated Woodward Valley Trail was, because the main vegetation along it is coastal scrub. This situation may allow it to recover more quickly from the Vision Fire. Probably the most noticeable shrub along this trail is the hardy coyote brush. It is a dioecious species, meaning that all the flowers on any one plant are of a single sex. (In most species, every flower has both stamens, which are male parts, and pistils, which are female parts.) If you hike here in the fall, when the female parts are flowering, you can easily see why this shrub is also called "fuzzy-wuzzy."

# Coast Camp and trails leading to it 🗼

## Coast Camp

*Facilities:* Water, toilets, picnic tables, grills, hitchrail.

*Regulations:* No dogs, no open fires.

Coast Camp, which is just a few hundred feet from attractive Santa Maria Beach, is protected by a sandy ridge from ocean winds.

The Vision Fire burned the camp pretty thoroughly, and it had to be closed for a few months, but it is now back in business and sporting green grass and wildflowers in spring.

Coast Camp is located on the site of the long-abandoned U Ranch, which was part of the Bear Valley (W) Ranch. The only remnant of ranching days is the large eucalyptus tree that stands sentinel over the beach entrance to the camp. Eucalyptus trees were popular among many ranchers in the 19th century, and in some of these abandoned ranches are the only surviving remembrances—as is the one at Kelham Beach.

*Some people look...*

*...others listen*

Actually, the shortest route to Coast Camp is to drive to the Limantour parking lot and walk 1½ miles southeast on the beach. This is an excellent idea for a leisurely afternoon picnic, but not a very enterprising backpack trip for a weekend. Another possibility is to start from the hostel and take the Coast Trail 2.8 miles down to the camp.

Whichever route you choose to Coast Camp, check a tide table or the newspaper before setting out, so you'll know when you can visit nearby Sculptured Beach, which is accessible only at low tide (see next chapter).

## Coast Trail north

The 8-mile route from the Bear Valley Visitor Center along the Bear Valley Trail and north on the Coast Trail is mostly level and very scenic.

Take the Bear Valley Trail for 4 miles and turn right on the Coast Trail. This old farm road runs along an ancient marine terrace now raised a couple of hundred feet above the ocean. If the day is clear, you can see the Farallon Islands and Point Reyes as you walk along it.

From the Sky Trail junction, 0.7 mile beyond the Bear Valley Trail, you will be walking along the burn zone. The effects of the fire are not quite so dramatic here as on the higher trails because the vegetation consists mainly of coastal scrub, which will regenerate more quickly than the lofty forests.

About a mile from the Bear Valley Trail is a junction with the access trail to Kelham Beach, under an old eucalyptus. This tree is the last remnant of Y Ranch, once part of the Bear Valley (W) Ranch.

The road continues along the headlands for about 2 miles. Shortly past a small gulch, the Woodward Valley Trail goes off to the right and the trail to Sculptured Beach to the left. If the tide is low enough you can visit this fascinating beach by making a short descent. The fantastically eroded, layered rocks offer marvelous opportunities for studying sea anemones and other tidepool life. The ochre cliffs, also obviously in the process of eroding, in places form bizarrely contoured canyons. As these cliffs are much too steep to climb, be sure to keep an eye on the tide.

When the tide is *really* low (minus) you can visit Secret Beach, south of Sculptured Beach.

At low tide you can proceed to Coast Camp on the beach—the most direct route. Or you can climb back up to the Coast Trail, which makes a **V** inland to cross Santa Maria Creek under willows and alders, then passes under a jutting rock formation and arrives at the camp.

From the camp you can proceed northwest to Limantour by walking about 1½ miles on the beach. Or you can continue northwest on the Coast Trail, passing the Fire Lane Trail on your right. The Coast Trail proper ends at the Point Reyes Hostel, 2.8 miles from Coast Camp.

# Limantour

*How to get there:* From the Bear Valley Visitor Center return to Bear Valley Road, turn left and drive north a mile to the Limantour Road turnoff on the left; follow it 8 miles to the end.

*Facilities:* Water, toilets, phone.

*Regulations:* Dogs on leash are allowed on Limantour Beach south of the parking lot; dogs are not allowed at all on the north side, which is a Research Natural Area.

Possibly the Limantour area acquired bad karma from its namesake. Estero de Limantour and its accompanying beach, sandspit, and road, are named for one of those outrageous characters who pop up from time to time in the annals of 19th century California. Jose Yves Limantour, a naturalized Mexican of French descent, loaded up the trading ship *Ayacucho* with luxury goods in 1841 and sailed from Mexico, aiming for San Francisco. Instead, he overshot the Golden Gate and ran aground on this sandspit. (This was the second shipwreck in Drakes Bay; the first was Cermeño's in 1595—see page 16.) Leaving his cargo on the beach, Limantour headed for San Francisco, toward which a friendly Indian had pointed the way. In the City he hired a ship's captain to recover the cargo, but gave him such poor

**A busy Sunday afternoon at Limantour Beach**

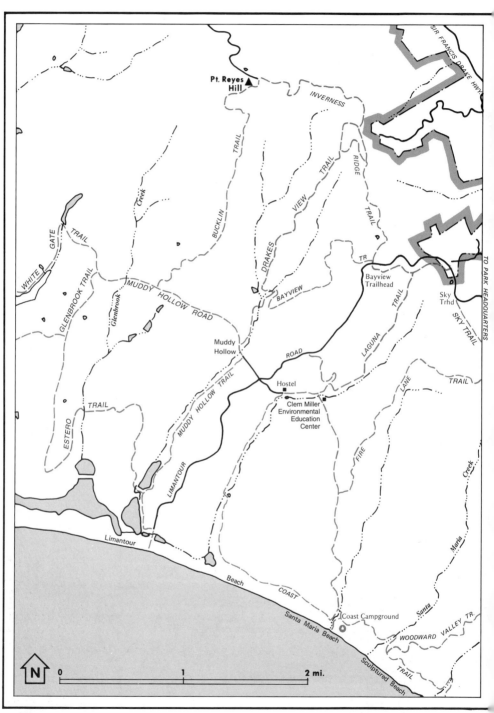

**THE LIMATOUR AREA**
**MAP 4**

LEGEND:  ══════ **Roads**
                 ‒‒‒‒‒‒ **Trail**
        ▬▬▬▬ **Park Bdy.**
        ✪ **Campground**

directions that the man ended up instead in Bolinas Lagoon. Next, Limantour himself led an overland party to fetch the treasure, but got lost. Finally John Reed, the first Mexican land grantee in Marin County, led Limantour to the goods.

In the 1850s Limantour claimed to have received from former governor Micheltorena grants of 600,000 acres, including half of San Francisco. Limantour pocketed between $250,000 and $500,000 from unsuspecting land buyers until 1858, when the Federal Government ruled that his documents were forgeries. By this time he had escaped to Mexico.

## The road to Limantour

As we noted on page 19, the north section of the Limantour Road was constructed in 1966, when the park planners were still thoroughly auto-oriented. Even then, environmentalists and downslope property owners objected to the construction of such a broad road on steep and unstable terrain so near the San Andreas Fault. The property owners filed suit to block its construction, but the suit was thrown out because—according to one of them—"the presiding federal judge was incapable of reading a map." During the storm of January 1982 slides occurred on the controversial new part of the road, and the Park Service closed the entire road to the public. Lack of funds prevented repair of the road for over a year, and in March 1983 another slide displaced a further 60-yard-long section of pavement.

For months afterwards extensive negotiations took place among the downslope property owners, the NPS, the Federal Highway Administration and representatives of then-Congresswoman Barbara Boxer. Eventually the road was rebuilt and it reopened in the fall of 1984.

The Vision Fire of October 1995 raced right down the Limantour area, on both sides of the road, until it reached the beach. All the vegetation was burned, but the firefighters managed to save the youth hostel and the Clem Miller Environmental Education Center, except for one outbuilding.

**The Clem Miller Environmental Center escaped the fire**

*Paul Backhurst*

In the first weeks after the fire, the scene along Limantour Road was one of eerie, gray devastation. But soon the vegetation started coming back, and after the plentiful rains of spring 1996 lush greenery covered the land. The most visible signs remaining of the fire along the road were the blackened bishop pines, which will reseed, and the burned stalks of coyote brush, which soon began to resprout from the roots. Cow parsnip, a large, vulgar-looking plant with white flowers, was one of the early species to come back.

By April 1996 the area near the Limantour parking lot sported a garden of wildflowers rivaling that of Chimney Rock: checkerbloom (wild hollyhock), iris, buttercups, sun cups, blue-eyed grass, coast lotus, lupine, Indian paintbrush, and pussy's ears (hairy star tulip).

## Limantour Beach and Muddy Hollow

It was the area above Limantour Beach that was scheduled for subdivision as Drakes Beach Estates in the 1950s. Early in 1961, George Dusheck reported in the San Francisco *News-Call-Bulletin*: "The stakes are up, with fluttering blue and red ribbons attached, on the half-acre homesites. Architects and engineers are at work on plans to dredge a small boat harbor, lay out a golf course, and erect a Carmel-type commercial development." This was one of the prospects that spurred conservationists and the National Park Service into action to establish the National Seashore. A few houses remain on the bluff above the beach; now they are residences of park personnel.

*Beautiful Limantour Beach inspires euphoria in some visitors*

In some respects Limantour Beach is the most idyllic in the Seashore. The ponds and marshes of its Protected Natural Area are a virtual paradise for birders and students of nature. A regular hiker in this area described it: "The receding tide revealed beautiful mazelike patterns formed by mudflats separated by channels of water: Christo couldn't have done as well!"

Beachcombers can frolic and wade along miles of clean white sand, enjoying on a clear day the view over Drakes Bay all the way from Double Point to Chimney Rock. Hikers can go south on the beach or over the bluffs to Coast Camp, and at low tide on to Sculptured Beach.

A good hike of about 4 miles round-trip is to Muddy Hollow and back. During the wet season it *is* muddy, so wear appropriate footgear. From the west end of the Limantour parking lot find the MUDDY HOL-LOW trailhead (sign). You walk along the edge of a marsh through coyote brush, and soon the sound of the waves behind you dims as you curve inland. You pass a causeway dividing a lagoon. Ducks frequent this lagoon, and in winter you may see some migrants from the north. The trail continues through the burn area to the Muddy Hollow parking lot.

## Trails leading from Limantour Road

It is apparent from a study of any trail map that the Limantour area offers abundant opportunities for all sorts of hikes—loop, round-trip, and shuttle. In the halcyon days of the 1970s a free shuttle bus ran regularly on weekends between Bear Valley and Limantour, stopping at trailheads along the way. The bus made it easy for not-so-energetic hikers to take mostly downhill trips or to visit Limantour Beach without driving. Alas, the bus is long gone, and we shall probably not see its like again unless some outdoors-loving billionaire decides to subsidize one. Nowadays people who want a downhill hike can arrange a car shuttle.

Because the vegetation along these trails will be constantly changing during the months and years after the October 1995 fire, I have not attempted to describe it in detail. Hikers and botanists can enjoy watching the natural succession of plant life as nature restores the area.

## From Sky Trailhead

The Sky Trail is the shortest route to Sky Camp, 1.2 miles. (Remember that if you plan to camp, you must first obtain a permit from the Bear Valley Visitor Center.) The trail begins under Douglas firs and ascends gently. Burned bishop pines soon become visible on the right. You pass junctions with the Fire Lane Trail and the Horse Trail and soon arrive at the camp (water, toilets). Most of the sites overlook the burn area stretching all the way to Drakes Bay.

At the entrance to the Sky Trailhead parking lot is the sign for the Bayview Trail, which runs to the Bayview Trailhead. Along the way, at 0.7 mile, the Laguna Trail begins its downhill run to the coast, passing the Clem Miller Environmental Education Center, which narrowly escaped the fire, losing only one outbuilding.

## From Bayview Trailhead

The Inverness Ridge Trail runs along the top of the ridge for 2.6 miles to Point Reyes Hill. It used to feature great views to east and west and a bishop-pine forest. The views remain but the bishop pines were among the first casualties of the October 1995 fire. Because these pines need fire to open their cones and reseed their habitat, it will be fascinating to watch their comeback along this trail.

## Muddy Hollow and South Estero Trail Loop
*A walk through the cradle of the Marin County dairy industry*

*How to get there:* Muddy Hollow Trailhead, about 6½ miles on Limantour Road from its start.

*Facilities:* No water along the route; no facilities.

*Regulations:* No dogs or bicycles.

*Note:* The walk description here is as the route was described *before* the October 1995 fire, which raged through much of the area. Hikers may be interested in comparing these trails before and after the fire.

This part of the Estero Trail has always been rather tricky to follow; hikers should check at one of the visitor centers to make sure it is passable.

This 5.5-mile walk traverses a rarely seen section of Point Reyes, where the ghosts of the original dairy ranches can perhaps be heard in the wind over the now-empty rangeland. Cows grazed the land for 120 years until it became part of the Phillip Burton Wilderness. It now affords lush habitat for birds and mammals (perhaps a mountain lion or two) and 360-degree vistas that include Limantour Estero, Drakes Bay, and Inverness Ridge.

You begin by passing through the gate at the north end of the parking area (you will return by the west gate on the other side of the lot). Within a few minutes a grand old stand of Monterey cypress looms on the right; here is the site of the Muddy Hollow ranch, founded by the Steele family around 1858. The Steeles came to the area from Ohio and settled in Sonoma County. Clara Steele, the story goes, milked a wild cow and with the milk made some cheese from a recipe she had found in a magazine. Sending the cheese to San Francisco, she discovered a ready market for dairy products in that growing city. Her husband and his siblings and cousin scanned the region for a suitable location for a dairy ranch, and found Point Reyes with its perennial grasses and wide-open spaces, proclaiming it "cow heaven."

On July 4, 1857, the Steeles rented ten thousand acres from Thomas Richards and soon established three dairies. They found immediate success in San Francisco markets, as fresh butter and cheese were in great demand. Until then, most dairy products had been shipped from the East Coast packed in brine; the resulting product on store shelves was less than desirable. From a schooner landing on Limantour Estero the family shipped their products, mostly cheese, and received their shipments of goods and furniture from the City. Family members built comfortable homes and equipped them with the trappings of their success. Employees manufactured fine cheeses using then-up-to-date technology (by today's standards primitive) in fine redwood ranch buildings.

Muddy Hollow, no doubt named for its physical characteristics during the winter, provided a good site for a dairy, although the hillsides exhibited a tendency toward brushiness. The ranch became a sheep ranch in the 1930s after the battle against brush was lost in the area. By 1960 all remnants of the ranch save the trees were gone. At the cypress trees is the junction of the Bayview Trail, which leads to Inverness Ridge.

Continue northwest on the Muddy Hollow Road, a dirt road that follows the original route from the Olema Valley to Point Reyes. Historians believe this route dates back to the Miwok Indians, and that Drake's party used it in 1579 to go from Drakes Beach to the Olema Valley. Muddy Hollow Road was the main pioneer route from Olema to Point Reyes until the alignment of what is now Sir Francis Drake Highway was adopted in 1873. Ranch owners widened and realigned this road in the 1950s, resulting in the large, eroding cuts along the way. During the 1960s and 1970s this was the proposed route of the controversial Muddy Hollow Road, which would have extended the new Limantour Road through this area to Point Reyes. Public outcry stopped the new Limantour Road at the summit of

Inverness Ridge.

As you approach the first summit look to the left (west) for two ponds, built in the 1950s for cattle; at the time the land was purchased for the park, it was slated for development, the two ponds figuring in the allure of the tract. The erosion on the next part of the trail, past the Bucklin Trail junction, is caused by the sloppily engineered roadworks. The next large drainage, marked by a large grove of alder trees, is Glenbrook Creek, a year-round stream. After entering another abused area—this one partly restored by

*Setting off through alders on the way to Muddy Hollow*

the Park Service—look for the Glenbrook Trail on your left and take it.

If you had continued straight ahead on the Muddy Hollow Road (not recommended, because the land is occupied) you would eventually have arrived at the Home Ranch, the headquarters ranch of the massive Shafter dairy empire that succeeded the Steeles. The brothers Shafter, Oscar and James, were influential attorneys who gained title to practically all of Point Reyes in the late 1850s, after a court battle with Thomas Richards and others. The Shafters and their in-law Charles Webb Howard developed most of the dairies on the peninsula during the 1860s, producing premium quality butter at more than thirty sites on the Point. The Home Ranch, built beginning in 1857, is intact and has been owned and occupied since 1929 by the Murphy family, who run beef cattle today. (Much of it narrowly escaped the 1995 fire; see p. 67.)

The Glenbrook Trail—actually an old ranch road—leads south, first uphill and then mostly level, through coyote brush; it offers a view of Inverness Ridge and, soon, of Limantour Estero. (Plentiful scats along the trail suggest an abundance of foxes.) At 0.6 mile from the Muddy Hollow Road you reach a junction with the Estero Trail. The current park sign here is a bit confusing, but it does indicate that if you were to take this trail west, eventually you would reach the estero and the site of the Steeles' wharf, where flat-bottomed schooners called regularly. The sign points east to Limantour Beach 2.0, but there is no trail in that direction! Instead, continue heading south on the old ranch road, which is now the Estero Trail. It makes a hairpin turn and after about ½ mile of descent enters a grove of eucalyptus trees marking the site of the New Albion Ranch, the Steeles' headquarters ranch. Here Isaac Steele superintended the family dairies, Muddy Hollow and Laguna ranches. The Steeles saw such success that they tried to buy the property from the Shafters. Rebuffed, they purchased the Año Nuevo Ranch near Pescadero instead, and became the Shafters' chief rivals as giants in the California dairy industry. New Albion, Muddy Hollow, and Laguna ranches were taken over by the Shafters and leased to tenant farmers.

The Shafters then leased the New Albion Ranch to such pioneer Point Reyesans as Martin Haggerty (who gave his name to Haggerty Gulch) and Pietro Scilacci, a prominent Swiss merchant in Point Reyes Station. During the 1920s and 1930s the ranch ended dairy production and began to produce artichokes (as well as serving as a fine spot for bootlegging). A school occupied one of the buildings for a quarter century. Roberts Dairy of San Rafael revitalized the dairy operation in the 1940s, but by the time Point Reyes National Seashore took over the property in 1971, decades of neglect had made the place unrestorable; so the first and perhaps most significant dairy ranch on Point Reyes was torn down.

After leaving the historic dairy site, the Estero Trail crosses Glenbrook Creek on an alder-shaded footbridge and traverses the hills to the lower part of Muddy Hollow Creek. Here a dam, built in the late 1950s, has created a lovely lake teeming with wildlife. This is the northern section of the infamous Drakes Bay Estates, a large subdivision that was well under way when Congress authorized the National Seashore in 1962. Had the development continued, the hills would be dotted with homes and the estero filled and crossed with roads with names like Nova Albion Way and Corsair Drive. As it was, about 18 houses were completed; all but three were removed by the Park Service.

You descend to the lake and soon cross the dam, under more alders. At the east end of the dam, turn left on the MUDDY HOLLOW TRAIL (sign). This level 1.4-mile walk leads back to the parking lot where you started.

To complete the history lesson, drive over to the Point Reyes Hostel at Laguna Ranch and have a look at the third Steele dairy ranch (after 4:30 P.M., please). Actually the Laguna Ranch was originally located downstream from its current site. It was moved in the 1870s and the main house at the hostel is the last remaining historic ranch house in this section of the park. Note the old addition off the kitchen, now used for a dining room: this was the Shafter School around the turn of the century, where generations of Muddy Hollow youngsters learned their ABCs.

*A modern Audubon painting the shorebirds of Limantour Estero*

The walk has taken you into the now-barren "cow heaven" that spurred the growth of a dairy industry that still dominates Marin County, a fact we can be glad of. It has been the dairy industry that has kept so much of Marin County in open space, and it is worth paying our respects to its origins.

# Along Sir Francis Drake Highway

## Mt. Vision and Point Reyes Hill

*How to get there:* From the Bear Valley Visitor Center take Bear Valley Road north, bear left onto Sir Francis Drake Highway, and continue on Drake through Inverness to the Pierce Point Road junction. Bear left to stay on Drake. The Mt. Vision turnoff is a mile beyond the junction. The 3-mile-long road up the mountain is narrow and twisting—not suitable for trailers.

*Facilities:* None except parking.

*Regulations:* No dogs.

Mt. Vision for decades was known primarily as a great place from which to view the countryside—and one, unlike Mt. Wittenberg, easily reached by car. After October 3, 1995, however, it will probably be notorious for decades as the starting place of the illegal campfire that ultimately burned over 12,000 acres and destroyed 45 homes (see Preface). Already this conflagration has become generally labeled "the Vision Fire."

Mt. Vision and nearby Point Reyes Hill still offer great views of the whole Point Reyes peninsula plus Mts. St. Helena, Diablo and Tamalpais. For years to come they will also offer great opportunities to watch the ecosystem regenerate from fire, and in particular to see a new bishop-pine forest growing along Inverness Ridge. The Mt. Vision area has always been a good place to see spring wildflowers within a short walk, and possibly the fire will encourage their profusion: not only the ubiquitous poppy and lupine, but also seaside daisy, baby-blue-eyes, harvest brodiaea, wild hollyhock, paintbrush, yarrow, and navarretia, popularly called skunkweed because of its odor.

Near the summit of Point Reyes Hill are some green spherical structures that appear to be extraterrestrial in origin. Actually

*Looking toward Mt. Wittenberg from the bushy trail near the summit of Mt. Vision*

65

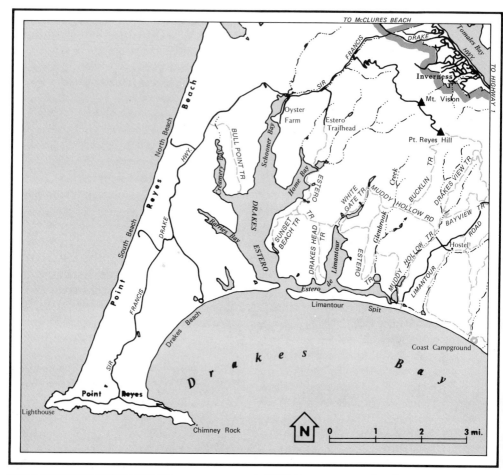

**ALONG SIR FRANCIS DRAKE HIGHWAY**
**MAP 5**

LEGEND:  ——— **Roads**
                     **Trail**
         ▬ ■ ▬ **Park Bdy.**
         ○ **Campground**

they have been installed by the Federal Aviation Administration to house a directional signal that guides planes to the San Francisco airport. They were not harmed by the fire. Signs near the FAA installation indicate various trails, with mileages, and may suggest possibilities for long hikes with a car shuttle along Inverness Ridge to the Bayview trailhead or downhill to Muddy Hollow or Limantour.

As you travel along Sir Francis Drake Highway heading toward the lighthouse, you will be passing by or through several of the oldest dairy ranches on the Point. Some of them are still flourishing and have been in the same families for generations.

As noted above, when the Shafters and Charles Webb Howard apportioned out their properties in the 1860s, they assigned them letters of the alphabet beginning at the south end of the Point with A and proceeding northward. Howard received A through G, which lie along the present route of Drake Highway. A line of eucalyptus on the north side of the highway marks the dividing line between G and H ranches. These trees were planted by Captain Henry Claussen, the son of a Danish immigrant from Schleswig-Holstein. Originally both father and son occupied G Ranch. In 1875 or 1876 Henry Claussen moved to E Ranch, where his family lived for over four decades. G Ranch is the site of a small cemetery where some of the Claussen family and some surfmen from the nearby lifesaving station are buried.

G Ranch's situation on the Pacific Ocean attracted overseas radio transmitting and receiving stations. RCA (now MCI) moved its Tomales Bay station here in 1929. The US Coast Guard has operated a station here since 1974. A bit to the south, on what used to be F Ranch, are AT&T's radio towers.

## Estero Trail and Drakes Head

*How to get there:* The road leading to the trailhead branches left from Drake Highway a short mile south of the road to Mt. Vision.

*Facilities:* Toilets at trailhead; no water along the route; the first ½ mile is wheelchair accessible.

The Estero Trail leads over open, gently rolling downs along the shore of Home Bay. It offers a grand opportunity to see wildlife. The mudflats bordering the bay and Drakes Estero are a feeding ground for a great number of shore and water birds, and on the way there you will also see land birds. You will almost certainly see cattle—since this area is still devoted to grazing—and probably deer, and perhaps harbor seals.

From the parking lot you can see Inverness Ridge, with Mt. Vision, Point Reyes Hill, and Mt. Wittenberg silhouetted. In the middle distance is the Home Ranch (alias Murphy, alias Drakes Bay Hereford), which park historian Dewey Livingston calls the oldest and best preserved of all the Point Reyes ranches. (According to the late Jack Mason, it was a prime area for rum-running during Prohibition.) The Vision Fire came close to destroying this ranch. However, ranchers and firefighters spent the better part of a day defending it. According to the *Point Reyes Light* of October 12: "The fire ultimately blackened 500 acres of the 3000-acre ranch. However, no buildings were damaged, and while the livestock were scared they were otherwise unscathed."

The Estero Trail used to begin by going uphill and then descending past an old cypress and skirting a former Christmas tree farm. Since the NPS has rerouted it to accommodate wheelchairs for the first ½ mile, the trail runs fairly level and then descends to go through the Christmas trees. Before descending, you can look over toward Mt. Vision and see the effects of the October 1995 fire—from this distance, mainly burned bishop-pine trees, since the rest of the vegetation is rapidly coming back. In the spring, iris abound on the early part of the trail. The new trail joins the old trail at a causeway over an inlet of Home Bay. A sign advises: DON'T TOUCH SEAL PUPS—MOTHER WILL ABANDON ANY PUPS TOUCHED.

The trail gradually ascends again to overlook the mudflats of Home Bay, Drakes Estero, and the Johnson Oyster Company's beds.

As you continue along the trail you may see great blue herons, egrets, godwits, willets, canvasbacks, buffleheads, ruddy ducks, and American widgeons, depending on the season and your luck. As you walk above the shore you might try to imagine the lively scenes here a hundred years ago, when the channel was

*The Estero Trail traverses moors and causeways above Home Bay*

navigable by schooner. A pier extended into Schooner Bay. Here the ships brought in feed and grain and picked up the very best butter, bound for the City. They also picked up live hogs. Historian Jack Mason noted, "If one fell in the water, it was a battle recovering him: Point Reyes hogs were, as we know, ferocious." Even larger schooners brought redwood lumber in from Santa Cruz.

After 2.4 miles the Estero Trail turns east, while the Sunset Beach Trail continues along Drakes Estero. This part of the Estero Trail is basically on old ranch roads marked with occasional NPS directional signs, running for 5½ miles to Limantour. It was fairly hard to follow *before* it got burned over by the Vision Fire, and it is difficult to predict what it will be like as it recovers.

For a scenic nonburned hike you might go 0.6 mile on the Estero Trail and then turn right (south) on the Drakes Head Trail. It runs 1.4 miles to end at a bluff overlooking Limantour Estero, with a panoramic view of Drakes Bay. A friend who hikes this trail regularly noted of a recent hike, in October: "We saw two white deer (grazing in the company of two deer of color). Looking down on the Estero de Limantour from Drakes Head, we saw four sea lions hauled out on sand flats, sand sharks, a great blue heron, brown pelicans diving, and scores of gulls."

In the 1920s and '30s the Drakes Head Ranch, which had previously been a dairy ranch, operated as a vegetable farm. A group of Italian farmers began successfully growing artichokes, and some Japanese farmers cultivated peas. When World War II broke out the Italians had to move away from the coast and the Japanese were sent to internment camps. By the mid-1950s the ranch was abandoned, and subsequently the owners tore down the remaining buildings.

## Johnson's Oyster Farm

| | |
|---|---|
| Address: | P.O. Box 68 |
| | Inverness, CA 94937 |
| Phone: | 669-1149 |
| Hours: | 8 A.M.–4:30 P.M. weekdays; 9 A.M.–4:30 P.M. weekends; closed Mondays. |

*How to get there:* The rugged road to the Oyster Farm leads left off Drake Highway 0.8 mile west of the turnoff to the Estero Trailhead, at a small sign. The narrow, rutted road leads a half mile to a jumble of houses, trailers, sheds, rusty machinery, and mounds and mounds of oyster shells. A distinctive odor pervades the air, especially at low tide. Frequently on weekends companionable groups of oyster-buyers chat as they wait their turn at the shed that houses the retail sales room.

Johnson's Oyster Farm has been a popular fixture on the Point Reyes peninsula since 1957. Its founder, the late Charlie Johnson, imported to Drakes Estero the Japanese method of oyster farming. The oyster seedlings are planted on strings hanging from platforms in the bay. Thus suspended, they are safe from their natural predators, such as crabs and starfish, which inhabit the mud and silt below. The oysterlings flourish on the plankton of the unpolluted bay until they are ready for harvesting 18 months later. This method vastly increases production: nearly 80 per cent of the oysters survive, as opposed to 20–30 per cent of oysters grown on muddy bottoms. Nowadays the seedlings are imported from Oregon rather than Japan.

In recent years the oyster farm, now run by Charlie's son Tom, has encountered problems. The county health department has complained that the company has moved in too many mobile homes for its septic system. The mobile homes house Johnson's employees. Most of them are low-income Hispanics who would not be able to find affordable housing elsewhere, and Johnson does not want to

**Sorting oysters from Drakes Estero at Johnson's Oyster Farm**

evict them. Johnson has tried to lease some adjoining land for an additional leachfield, but the Park Service takes a dim view of giving up land to a nonagricultural commercial enterprise.

PRNS would like to retain the oyster farm as a tenant. At present the Johnsons are negotiating with the Park Service and the county to cut down the number of trailers on the property. Meanwhile the oyster farm is still operating and selling oysters to the public.

## Bull Point Trail

*How to get there:* The trailhead is on the left side of Drake Highway, about 2 miles beyond the road to the Oyster Farm, just past the AT&T radio towers on the right.

*Facilities:* Small parking lot; no water or toilets.

Just north of the trailhead are a few forlorn old cypress and eucalyptus trees that mark the site of the original F Ranch buildings, now all destroyed. Hard as it is to imagine now, F Ranch was once a flourishing enterprise that contained a store, the post office for the Point, and a busy schooner landing on Schooner Bay.

The Bull Point Trail might be considered a shorter version of the Estero Trail: it is fairly level and mostly treeless, and it offers a good opportunity to see wildlife, both birds and animals; also plenty of bovine life. It is, like so many of the trails in the area, an old farm road.

From the trailhead the trail runs mostly flat and open, through lupines. Then it goes gently uphill above Creamery Bay. Along the way we saw several deer, a few egrets, and lots of cows. In a short 2 miles the trail peters out on a small beach at Drakes Estero; this looks like a good spot to see harbor seals hauled out, although none happened to be there on the day we hiked it.

On our return trip we did encounter a bull, fittingly enough. He was standing athwart the trail and obviously had no intention of moving. We prudently (or cravenly) made a wide circle around him by going cross-country. Fortunately the terrain here is so level and open that it is easy to make a cross-country detour.

## Point Reyes Beach, North and South

*How to get there:* The road to Point Reyes Beach North is on the right, 2.7 miles west of the Oyster Company road. The road to Point Reyes Beach South is 2½ miles farther along Drake. (The road to Drakes Beach begins on the left, between the two Point Reyes Beach roads.)

*Facilities:* Water; restrooms at North Beach (the ones at South Beach were destroyed by arson in 1993 but are scheduled to be replaced in 1997); picnic tables; dogs permitted on 6-foot leash.

*Regulations:* No swimming or wading because of the dangerous surf.

Point Reyes Beach, also called Ten Mile Beach or the Great Beach, is one long beach with two automobile entrances. It is one of the best places in the Bay Area to shake off urban malaise.

This wild and windy strand offers an exhilarating opportunity to run for miles. You can also walk the dog, or fish for perch, or make sculptures out of the abundant driftwood. During the winter you can watch for migrating whales.

If you come here on a foggy or stormy day, you can readily understand why

**A ramble on Point Reyes Beach with only seagulls for company**

so many shipwrecks took place on this beach, even after the lighthouse was built in 1870. The Coast Guard operated a lifesaving station here from 1890 until 1927, when it was moved to more sheltered Drakes Bay.

The local ranchers on occasion took part in rescue operations—as in 1861, when Carlisle S. Abbott saved all but one of the crew of the *Sea Nymph* by lassoing them as they struggled in the surf and tugging them ashore. The ranchers also took advantage of the salvage law to pick up cargo from abandoned ships. In 1874 the same Captain Claussen who planted the eucalyptus lane retrieved the figurehead of the New Zealand ship *Warrior Queen* and kept it prominently displayed on his ranch for many years. In 1885 Claussen swam to the abandoned English ship *Haddingtonshire*, rigged up a breeches buoy, and salvaged some of her cargo.

You can learn more about Point Reyes shipwrecks when you visit the lighthouse.

## Drakes Beach

*How to get there:* The turnoff is 2 miles south of the turnoff to Point Reyes Beach North.

*Facilities:* Water; restrooms and dressing rooms, picnic tables, grills.

*Regulations:* No dogs.

The Ken C. Patrick Visitor Center was expanded in 1991, thanks largely to the Point Reyes National Seashore Association, which provided funding. The center is named for the first NPS ranger ever to be killed in the line of duty: in 1973 he was shot by deer poachers on the slopes of Mt. Vision. (Mt. Vision, like the Limantour Road, seems to have more than its share of bad karma.) The chief poacher was sentenced to life imprisonment; the other two turned state's evidence and received lesser sentences.

The center is definitely worth a visit if you're there when it's open. It contains an aquarium, a whale skeleton, and other exhibits devoted to the marine environment and maritime exploration. Hours: 10 A.M.–noon and 12:30–5 P.M. weekends and holidays; closed weekdays (phone 669-1250).

The Drakes Beach Café is definitely several cuts above the usual park concession; in fact, it offers a good excuse not to bother packing a picnic when visiting Drakes Beach. The café features local specialties, high-grade ingredients, and home cooking. Hours: 10 A.M.–6 P.M. Thursday through Monday; more frequently during summer (phone 669-1297).

Looking at this tranquil, isolated spot, one would hardly guess that it is the center of a historical controversy that has aroused violent passions not only in California but around the world, and is still making headlines more than 400 years after the event that started it. To summarize briefly: In 1579, Francis Drake (who had not yet been knighted), having liberated a good deal of treasure from the Spaniards in the New World, was sailing along the California coast in search of a sheltered harbor where he could careen his weather-beaten ship, the *Golden Hinde*, and make the repairs necessary for the voyage across the Pacific to the Orient and eventually back to England. On June 17 he found such a harbor; he brought the ship in and stayed until July 23.

Almost all we know about his visit is what we learn from an account presumably written by his chaplain, Francis Fletcher, because Drake's own log has not been seen since he presented it to Queen Elizabeth I upon his return. And even what we learn from Fletcher is secondhand: the first account relying on his journal was Richard Hakluyt's *The Famous Voyage of Sir Francis Drake into the South Sea*, published in 1589; the second was *The World Encompassed by Sir Francis Drake*, published in 1628—nearly 50 years after the event.

According to Fletcher, the harbor was "convenient and fit" but the climate

*The attractive Kenneth C. Patrick visitor center at Drakes Beach has ample parking space*

was one of "thick mists and most stinking fogs." Drake called the place Nova Albion, partly because its white banks and cliffs reminded him of home. A large number of friendly Indians came to greet them and give them presents. Before leaving, Drake ceremonially took possession of the land in the name of Queen Elizabeth I, and nailed on a post a "plate of brass" inscribed to that effect.

Several generations of historians, both professional and amateur, have argued fiercely over just where the *Golden Hinde* landed. In addition to Fletcher's account, they have a sketch map to go by: published in 1589 by a Flemish cartographer, Jodocus Hondius, it purports to show the port of Nova Albion.

This map is just as frustratingly vague as Fletcher's description, and at one time or another has been claimed to represent almost every bay in central and northern California. The majority of historians has long favored Drakes Bay as the landing place, but an articulate minority champions the northwest shore of San Francisco Bay. Bolinas Lagoon and Bodega and Tomales bays also have their partisans. Recently an Englishman has come up with the theory that Drake actually landed in Coos Bay, Oregon!

When a picnicker found what appeared to be Drake's original plate of brass near San Quentin Point in 1936, far from settling the question, it aroused even more controversy. If the plate were genuine, as metallurgical tests seemed to indicate, it would be powerful evidence in favor of San Francisco Bay. However, another man then came forth to state that he had picked up the plate near Drakes Bay and carried it around in his car for three years before finally throwing it out near San Quentin Point. And so the argument simmered on. Meanwhile, the plate of brass was ensconced in The Bancroft Library at the University of California, Berkeley, as one of that institution's most prized treasures.

In 1974, while some Drake fans were sailing from Plymouth, England, across the Atlantic in a painstakingly authentic replica of the *Golden Hinde*, the Drake controversy heated up again in the US. The California Historical Society devoted the entire fall issue of its *Quarterly* to a vigorous three-way debate among partisans of Drakes Estero, Bolinas Lagoon, and San Quentin Cove as the landing place. Shortly thereafter, the prestigious historian Samuel Eliot Morison branded the plate of brass a fake, and suggested it might have been produced as an undergraduate prank.

Even before Morison's attack, the new Director of The Bancroft Library, Dr. James D. Hart, anticipating intensified interest in Drake as the quadricentennial of his landing approached, had arranged for further investigation of the plate. Techniques of metallurgy had become considerably more sophisticated in the nearly 40 years since the plate had been found. After scientists at Berkeley and Oxford subjected the plate to exhaustive analyses, Hart announced in 1977 that the tests strongly suggested that it was composed of modern metal rolled and cut in ways unknown in Drake's time. He added, with scholarly understatement but great prescience, that his report was "made with the recognition that this will probably not be accepted everywhere as the definitive or conclusive word on the subject."

The Bancroft report put the Elizabethan navigator on the front pages again, and the quadricentennial festivities kept him there. On June 16, 1979, the Sir Francis Drake Quadricentennial Committee of the Marin Coast Chamber of Commerce dedicated a bronze plaque near the south edge of the Drakes Beach parking lot, which reads: "On June 17, 1579, Captain Francis Drake sailed his ship *Golden Hinde* into the Gulf of the Farallones and the Bay that now bears his name. He sighted these white cliffs and named the land Nova Albion." A day earlier the Golden Gate National Recreation Area had dedicated a more noncommittal marker on Vista Point at the north end of the Golden Gate Bridge, stating "Historians have not yet agreed whether Drake's Marin County anchorage was in Drakes Estero, Bolinas Lagoon, or San Francisco Bay." The California Historical Resources Com-

mission couldn't agree to put a plaque *any*where.

The quadricentennial celebration was barely over when a completely novel argument enlivened the Drake controversy. As we noted on p. 16, Cermeño's Manila galleon was wrecked by a storm in Drakes Bay in 1595, and shards from her cargo of Ming porcelain subsequently turned up in excavations of Coast Miwok villages. Early in 1980 two scholars of porcelain studied almost 600 shards from the shores of Drakes Bay and concluded that they came from two entirely different shipments—one of them probably Drake's, since he was known to have looted some Ming porcelain from Spanish ships.

*The quadricentennial of Drake's landing attracts the navigator's admirers to the visitor center*

Anyone who has spent much time with Drakologists is well aware that it will take more than a few hundred pieces of china to settle this controversy. Much more incontrovertible evidence will be required—something like Drake's original log, if it should one day turn up in a long-neglected corner of the Tower of London or the Public Records Office, and if the paper, the ink, the handwriting, and the wording could be certified as authentic by chemists, graphologists, and linguists.

Even if you're firmly convinced that Drake really landed somewhere else, you'll still enjoy hiking up and down Drakes Beach, or just sunbathing on it. It's often less windy than the ocean beaches, and the quieter surf permits wading. You can also enjoy a leisurely stroll to examine the various Drake monuments that have been erected over the years. (When the visitor center is open, you can pick up a little guide to them.)

The oldest one is a rough-hewn granite cross under some Monterey pines and cypresses just north of the small picnic area adjoining the parking lot. Erected by the Sir Francis Drake Association of San Francisco in 1946, it commemorates the first Anglican church service held in what is now the United States, at which Chaplain Fletcher, the voyage's annalist, presided along with Drake.

At the south edge of the parking lot is the bronze plaque placed by the Sir Francis Drake Quadricentennial Committee of the Marin Coast Chamber of Commerce on June 16, 1979, and dedicated by the Lord Bishop of London.

To reach the other monuments you walk east along the beach. (It is occasionally flooded at high tide. On weekends the visitor center posts tide tables.) The sand on Drakes Beach is constantly shifting with the tides and the seasons, and rocky shelves that may project three or four feet above the beach at one time you visit may be almost completely covered with sand another time.

A little over a mile from the parking lot, past the second bluff, when you see riffles in a channel ahead of you, look left to find a post about 12 feet high and less than ¼ mile away. You walk toward it (in spring, through mauve and violet lupine and golden fiddleneck) to find two more monuments. The old anchor, suggested by Lord Louis Mountbatten and donated by the Royal Navy, was erected by the Drake Navigators Guild in 1954. Its accompanying sign states in no uncertain terms: "June 17, 1579, Francis Drake landed in this cove and here repaired his ship." Below the anchor a gray-black granite plaque placed by the guild in 1979 is somewhat more hesitant: "This cove is believed by many scholars to be the site of Sir Francis Drake's California harbor."

I had walked here alone late one afternoon to study the monuments. As I was transcribing their inscriptions, and musing on the enigmas of history, I was startled by a gunshot-loud SPLAT behind me. Whirling around, I discovered a harbor seal which had just flopped inelegantly into the estero and was swimming toward me. Behind him, lounging on a sandspit, was a colony of his fellows.

I walked through the tufts of bushy lupine to the shore and along it, followed in the water by the inquisitive seal. The mouth of the estero at low tide seemed barely deep enough to admit even a canoe. We know, however, that ocean-going schooners regularly navigated it during the 19th century, so presumably Drake could have done so in the 16th.

It would indeed be exciting to have the Drake mystery solved beyond the shadow of a doubt, but then the great navigator

*Lord Louis Mountbatten suggested that the British Navy contribute this anchor to mark the entrance to Drakes Estero*

might vanish forever from the front pages of our newspapers—and I, for one, find him much more agreeable than most of the 20th century phenomena I encounter there.

Meanwhile. . .in recent years, attempts have been made to find Cermeño's sunken Manila galleon *San Agustin*, which must lie somewhere in Drakes Bay (see p. 16). After the storms of 1982 and '83 the NPS Submerged Cultural Research unit investigated the bay and found the steamship *Pomo*, which went down in 1913 with no loss of life, and a couple of schooners—but no *San Agustin*. In the late 1980s a swashbuckling marine archeologist and treasure-seeker from Florida, Robert Marx—sometimes called by the press "The Indiana Jones of shipwrecks"— after years of wrangling with the bureaucracies of the state and federal governments obtained permission to search the bay. But even if he had found the *San Agustin* there is some doubt as to whether the state, the NPS, or the salvager would have had jurisdiction over the vessel.

As noted above (p. 16), an archeological team from Sonoma State University, sponsored by the Drake Navigators Guild, is trying to find the remains of Cermeño's camp, which might give a clue to the location of the galleon. At this point the *San Agustin* presents a tantalizing mystery to historians rather like the *Golden Hinde*, albeit on a smaller scale.

### Recommended reading

Hanna, Warren, *Lost Harbor: The Controversy over Drake's California Anchorage*. Berkeley: University of California Press, 1979.
*The Plate of Brass Reexamined*. Berkeley: The Bancroft Library, University of California, 1977.
*The Plate of Brass Reexamined: Supplement*. Berkeley: The Bancroft Library, University of California, 1979.

The periodical literature is too abundant to cite here. Anyone who is interested should consult back files of the California Historical Society's journal, particularly the issue for Fall 1974.

## Chimney Rock Trail

*How to get there:* The turnoff is on the left, 3½ miles beyond the road to Point Reyes Beach South. On the way to the turnoff you will pass right through C Ranch (Spaletta), B Ranch (J.H. Mendoza), and A Ranch (Nunes). From the turnoff a narrow road leads a mile to the main parking lot, passing another small parking lot along the way. The lifeboat station is just below the main parking lot.

*Facilities:* Toilet at main parking lot.

*Regulations:* No dogs; stay inside fences on the crumbly, eroding cliffs. Not a regulation, just a piece of advice: bring along an extra sweater, jacket, or parka because it is *always* windy on the Chimney Rock promontory.

Even after the lighthouse was constructed in 1870, shipwrecks continued on the foggy peninsula. In 1888 the US Life-Saving Service purchased land on South Beach and built an elegant house (since, alas, destroyed) for the captain and some of the crew, and a boathouse which began operating in 1890. In 1915 the Life-Saving Service was incorporated into the US Coast Guard, which in 1927 built a new station on Drakes Bay that would be more sheltered than the storm-ridden South Beach. The new facility included a pier with tracks for two motorized boats, plus a New England-style house for the chief.

The lifeboat station operated until 1968. (The Coast Guard had opened a more advanced facility on Bodega Bay in 1963.) The NPS took over the station and restored it; in 1990 it was designated a National Historic Landmark. At present it is open to the public one weekend day per month: check the Seashore schedule at the visitor centers for "Open House/Lifeboat Station." Commercial fishing boats frequent the bay offshore, especially during the salmon season.

A path leads from the main parking lot across windswept pasture to the promontory above Chimney Rock. On a clear day you can see down the coast all the way to San Francisco. To the north, the cliffs behind Drakes Bay resemble the White Cliffs of Dover more closely from this vantage point than from anywhere else in the Seashore.

A unique attraction here is

*At low tide the rocks of Drakes Beach are a good place to look for tidepool creatures*

the profusion of wildflowers in the spring. In the short mile between the parking lot and the overlook on one April day we noted owl's clover, tidy tips, sun cups, pussy's ears, baby-blue-eyes, phacelia, iris, wild hollyhock, paintbrush, lupine, and mule ears—and we probably missed some others.

A more recent attraction is the congregation of elephant seals at the foot of the promontory during their breeding season, January through March. Add to these attractions the possibility of seeing whales on their northward migration, and you can understand why a traffic jam may occur on the narrow road to the parking lot. As this book goes to press, the Park Service is considering instituting some kind of shuttle from South Beach or Drakes Beach during spring weekends.

If the view of the white cliffs has reminded you of Sir Francis Drake, you can search out yet another monument to the great navigator. Beside the stairs leading to the front door of the lifeboat station a bronze plaque declares unequivocally, "Francis Drake landed on these shores and took possession of the country, calling it Nova Albion." This monument was installed on June 17, 1950 (the 371st anniversary of Drake's landing) by the Yerba Buena chapter of E Clampus Vitus, a fraternal organization originally founded during Gold Rush days that is interested in California history.

## The lighthouse

*How to get there:* Continue on Drake Highway to its end, about 21 miles beyond Bear Valley Visitor Center.

During whale migration season—approximately January–March—the Park Service has run a free shuttle bus between Drakes Beach or South Beach and the lighthouse parking lot. The advent of elephant seals on the beaches beneath Chimney Rock and the lighthouse has attracted more visitors than ever, and the Seashore may have to reinstitute some kind of shuttle on weekends to prevent complete gridlock.

About ¾ mile past the Chimney Rock turnoff, or ¼ mile before you reach the lighthouse parking lot, a small parking area on the left (south) side of the road gives access to the sea-lion overlook.

*Facilities:* Water, restrooms; visitor center open 10 A.M.–5 P.M. Thursday through Monday; lighthouse stairs open 10 A.M.–4:30 P.M. those days except when very foggy or windy. Disabled visitors should call ahead to the visitor center to find out about access (669-1534).

*Regulations:* No dogs; stay on established trails and do not venture on hazardous cliffs.

The many shipwrecks on Point Reyes made a lighthouse a virtual necessity. Congress appropriated the money for it in 1852, but a protracted legal battle with the Shafter-Howard clan over the price of the land delayed construction for 18 years, during which period several more ships were wrecked. Finally, in 1870, the lighthouse was constructed, halfway down the 600-foot cliff. Why not at the top? Because while the Government was wrangling over the purchase of the Point Reyes land, the lighthouse service went ahead and built one at Point Bonita, north of the Golden Gate. They placed this light atop the cliff, but soon discovered that too often it was obscured by fog. Hence when they came to install the light at Point Reyes, they put it halfway down the cliff, even though this site greatly increased the expense and difficulty of constructing it and subsequently provisioning it. As a result, to visit the lighthouse you have to walk down stairs equivalent to a 30-story building—which isn't so bad, except that you then have to walk back up.

The old light, which was imported from France, is an extraordinarily complex and beautiful piece of machinery. (You can pick up a diagram of it at the visitor center.) Using only the light from four oil-burning wicks, its intricate lens containing over a thousand pieces of glass enabled it to be seen 24 nautical miles out to sea.

Despite the light, and the installation of a foghorn in 1871, ships continued to be wrecked. Part of the problem was fog: Point Reyes is the foggiest spot on the

*The stairs to the lighthouse have several platforms where visitors can rest and watch for whales*

*National Park Service photo by Dewey Livingston*

Pacific Coast, and is second only to Nantucket Island in the whole United States. Another problem was that mariners mistook Point Reyes for the Golden Gate. One reason the shipwrecks produced relatively few fatalities was the installation of the Coast Guard Life-Saving Service, which operated on Point Reyes Beach from 1888 until 1927, when it was moved to Drakes Bay. Oddly enough, one of the most serious wrecks on the Point involved not a ship but a United Airlines DC-3 which crashed in 1938, killing five persons.

Life at the lighthouse in its early days was not easy. Just provisioning the place was a major undertaking, as you can imagine when you walk down the stairs to the light. Considering the keepers' isolation from society, the terrible weather they had to contend with, and the din of the foghorn—sometimes going on for days—it is not surprising that insubordination and drunkenness were frequent, and that in 1889 an assistant "went crazy and was handed over to the constable in Olema."

Since those days both the light and the foghorn have benefited from technical improvements that made duty easier for the keepers who manned them. In 1975 a new light was installed, one that is automated by a computer. The old light is still operable, however, just in case the computer should ever fail. The Coast Guard closed the lighthouse to the public in 1967 because it lacked personnel to oversee visitors on the then-hazardous stairs. After automation, the Coast Guard turned the lighthouse over to the National Park Service, which reopened it to the public in 1977.

The road from the parking lot to the lighthouse leads past cypress trees and wildflowers, and on clear days affords a view of the Great Beach and north to Bodega Head. Of course in winter you will be keeping your eyes open for migrating whales. The search for whales can also occupy you during the long trek down the stairs, and the even longer one back up. The Park Service has considerately provided rest stops at intervals. When the whales are not running, you can entertain yourself by studying the myriad of succulents and wildflowers along the stairs and the colorful lichen on the rocks. The rocks themselves near the visitor center represent what geologist Alan Galloway refers to as "fine exposures of coarse Paleocene conglomerate" and "interesting sedimentary structures."

*The Fresnel lens of the old lighthouse, made in Paris in 1867, has over a thousand pieces of glass*

# Along Pierce Point Road 🗼

Although the road is officially called *Pierce Point*, the point itself appears on most maps as *Tomales*. The road is named for Solomon Pierce, who in 1858 bought 220 acres on the point and established a model dairy ranch, described on  p. 88.

Pierce Point Road runs across some of the wildest country on the Point Reyes peninsula. After you leave the bishop pines of Tomales Bay State Park, there are few trees and you can see for miles over the moors and out to sea. One might consider the landscape almost desolate were it not for the occasional substantial-looking ranch houses and the multitude of cattle. The pungent odor of manure often drifts through the car window. This is good birding country: crows, ravens, and vultures are much in evidence, and hawks perch on the fences and telephone poles near the road. Often they will let you get surprisingly close to them.

## Tomales Bay State Park

Phone: 669-1140

*How to get there:* From Inverness drive west and then south on Sir Francis Drake Highway for 2½ miles to Pierce Point Road and turn right onto it. The main entrance to the park is a little over a mile from Drake Highway.

If all you want to do in the park is hike, not swim or picnic, you can some-times find a (free) parking place in the clearing 350 yards south of the main entrance; the Jepson trail, described below, takes off from here, and so does the 3-mile-long trail to Shell Beach.

Shell Beach, although part of the state park—in fact, the oldest part of it—is separated from the park's other beaches by a patch of private land. In the summer of 1980 a youth conservation group constructed a trail linking Shell with the other beaches, and it is described at the end of this section. Drivers, however, must still approach Shell by the traditional route: From Inverness, drive north on Drake Highway, turn right on Camino del Mar (about a mile from "downtown" Inverness), and follow it to the small parking lot at its end. From here you have to walk about a quarter mile through oak and madrone woodland to the beach. Actually, Shell consists of two beaches. To reach Shell II you walk another quarter mile north of Shell I. Both beaches are extremely attractive and are much favored by the local residents.

*Facilities:* Water, restrooms and dressing rooms, picnic tables, grills; about 20 bicycle campsites. Hand-carried boats may be put in the water away from the swimming beaches. Map available from ranger station for a small price.

*Regulations:* Park generally open during daylight hours; day-use fee $5 per car, $4 for seniors 62 and over; each dog $1 (except guide dogs free); hike/bike campsites $3 per night. Dogs are allowed only in the upper picnic area and must be kept on leash at all times.

81

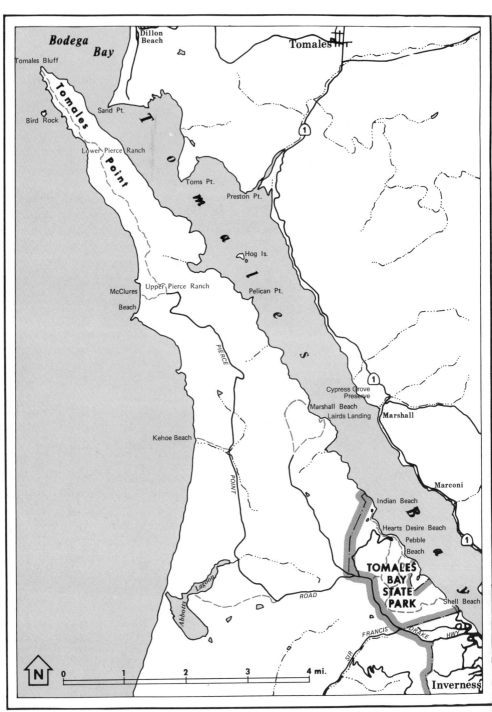

Bodega
Bay

Dillon
Beach

Tomales

Tomales Bluff

Bird Rock

Sand Pt.

Lower Pierce Ranch

Toms Pt.

Preston Pt.

Hog Is.

Upper Pierce Ranch

Pelican Pt.

McClures
Beach

PIERCE

Cypress Grove
Preserve

Marshall Beach
Lairds Landing

Marshall

Kehoe Beach

POINT

Marconi

Indian Beach

Hearts Desire Beach

Pebble
Beach

TOMALES
BAY
STATE
PARK

Shell Beach

Abbotts Lagoon

ROAD

FRANCIS

SIR

DRAKE

HWY

Inverness

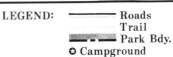

N

0     1     2     3     4 mi.

**ALONG PIERCE POINT ROAD**
# MAP 6

LEGEND: ———— Roads
           Trail
━━━ ━ Park Bdy.
✪ Campground

The earliest Spanish explorers sailing along the coast—Sebastian Vizcaino in 1603 and Lt. Juan Francisco de la Bodega y Cuadro in 1775—thought that Tomales Bay was actually a great river, *rio grande*. It was not until 1793, when Captain Juan B. Matute explored it more thoroughly, that the Spanish realized that it was actually a long bay.

Tomales Bay State Park antedates Point Reyes National Seashore by a full decade. In fact, it was the threat of private development on the bayfront here that first spurred conservationist militance in the Point Reyes area. In 1945 a group led by the Marin Conservation League purchased 185 acres at Shell Beach for $30,000 (about what one quarter acre of unimproved land sells for in the Inverness area now; obviously, they got there at the right time). In 1951 a combination of private contributors, conservationist groups, and the state purchased another 840 acres, and a year later the state took over both parcels as a park. It remains a sort of enclave within the National Seashore.

This charming park is sometimes a sunny refuge when the rest of the peninsula is fogged in. Its small, sheltered beaches are a pleasant contrast to the windswept ones on the rest of the peninsula, and for swimmers Tomales Bay is milder and warmer than Drakes Bay—let alone the Pacific Ocean. (There is no lifeguard service, however.) The picnic area is unusually attractive, containing many tables screened by lush foliage and offering splendid views across the bay.

From the parking lot at Hearts Desire Beach, short trails lead north over the forested bluffs to Indian Beach and south to Pebble Beach. Children will enjoy these walks from beach to beach, and will see why the Coast Miwok Indians were

*Picnickers at one of the pleasant sites of Tomales Bay State Park*

so fond of this area. Three simple teepees now adorn Indian Beach. Fishing and clamming were popular with the Indians, and still are; but unlike the original inhabitants, you will have to obtain a fishing license before you arrive.

## Jepson-Johnstone loop

A delightful loop hike of a bit under 3 miles can be made by combining the Jepson and Johnstone trails. This hike is enjoyable at almost any time of year, in almost any weather short of a driving rainstorm. To start it from Hearts Desire Beach, take the trail leading to Pebble Beach. It traverses the picnic area and just before actually reaching the beach connects with the Johnstone Trail (named for the late Bruce Johnstone, a leading Marin conservationist). The trail ascends gradually through luxuriant shrubbery, ferns, and picturesque trees. The Park Service has recycled some of its former signs to create footbridges over occasional steamlets.

A mile from Pebble Beach, the Johnstone Trail arrives at a gravel road. If you go uphill on the road for ¼ mile you come to a locked vehicle gate and the unofficial free parking lot mentioned above. To finish your loop back to Hearts Desire Beach, take the (signed) Jepson Trail. This trail is named for the late botanist Willis Linn Jepson, founder of the UC School of Forestry and author of the monumental *Manual of the Flowering Plants of California*. The trail goes through the Jepson Memorial Grove of bishop pines. As we noted in the Introduction, the Point Reyes peninsula is one of the very few places where this ancient species of pine flourishes. Now that so many of the bishop-pine trees on Inverness Ridge have burned down, this may be one of the last places to see a virgin bishop-pine forest. Occasional well-sited benches invite the hiker to rest and contemplate the view through pines, oaks, and madrones over Tomales Bay. After a mile in the verdant forest, you arrive again at the main parking lot.

For a longer hike, you can try the continuation of the Johnstone Trail, which connects Hearts Desire and Shell beaches, bypassing

*Jogging through the forest on the Jepson Trail*

the private land between them. This is a hike of about 4 miles each way (not counting the half mile to the Shell Beach parking lot). It offers a good opportunity for a car shuttle.

You can get on this trail either by continuing west on the Johnstone Trail until it turns south, or crossing the paved road at the end of the Jepson Trail. If you don't wish to enjoy the amenities of the state park proper, you can shorten the approach by parking in the unofficial parking lot just before the park entrance and walking down the paved road a short distance to the signed Johnstone Trail heading south on your right.

This trail is heavily vegetated—so heavily, in fact, that from time to time the shrubbery has to be trimmed. Shortly beyond the paved road is a large patch of ledum downhill on the left. Other plentiful flora along the trail include salal, swordfern, honeysuckle, monkeyflower, coffeeberry, and huckleberry. The trail contours at an elevation of about 500 feet. Once in a while a break in the forest permits views of Tomales Bay.

*A covey of California quail beside Pierce Point Road*

After a couple of miles the trail begins to descend gradually through tanoak and madrone, and then comes out at Shell Beach II. If you're hiking in the other direction, you can pick up this trail at the north end of the beach, near the garbage cans.

## Marshall Beach

*How to get there:* The road leading to the beach begins just beyond the road to Tomales Bay State Park, at a sign L RANCH. After emerging from a short section of forest, the rough (*very* rough in spots) road runs over moors offering a superb view of Abbotts Lagoon, the Pacific Ocean, and Tomales Bay. The buildings of L Ranch are barely visible in the distance. This road was the main route to Pierce Point until the present road there was built in 1941. After 2½ miles you arrive at a primitive parking lot. From here a trail leads 1¼ miles down to the beach. Be sure to close cattle gates after you.

*Facilities:* Toilets, picnic tables at beach.

*Regulations:* No dogs, camping, or motor vehicles.

The beach is named for rancher Robert Marshall, who bought the property in 1960—not for the Marshall brothers who founded the town across Tomales Bay. The first part of the trail continues to offer great views over Tomales Bay. In spring, common linanthus is abundant along the edge of the trail. Eventually the trail descends rather steeply to a grove of cypresses and the small, protected beach. Just across the bay are the Victorian buildings of Audubon Canyon Ranch's Cypress Grove Preserve.

(A personal note: I've been to this beach by foot and I've been there by boat, and by boat is better. Try to strike up an acquaintance with someone who keeps a boat moored on Tomales Bay!)

Just south of Marshall Beach is Lairds Landing. Originally this was the site of a Coast Miwok village. In 1859 the Laird brothers leased the land, subsequently K Ranch, from the Shafters and established a prosperous dairy operation. They shipped their cheese to San Francisco from a wharf at the landing. After the Lairds moved to the other shore of Tomales Bay in 1866, a succession of tenants and owners occupied K Ranch until the NPS purchased it in the 1970s. The late artist Clayton Lewis, who had moved to the landing in 1964, remained there on a special permit from the NPS until his death in 1995. He renovated some of the old Miwok buildings and maintained an art studio. Some of his friends have broached the idea of establishing a nonprofit foundation in his home to study the biology of Tomales Bay. The NPS has put this proposal on hold for the time being.

## Abbotts Lagoon

*How to get there:* The small parking lot is 2 miles beyond the turnoff to Tomales Bay State Park on the Pierce Point Road.

*Facilities:* Toilets at parking lot. Swimming is possible in the lagoon, but not the ocean. The lagoon is large enough that you can canoe in it, if you're willing to portage the canoe a few hundred feet from the parking lot and subsequently over the natural dam separating the two parts of the lagoon.

*Regulations:* No dogs, camping, or motor vehicles.

The Abbott brothers were ranchers here in the 1860s. It was one of them, Carlisle, who saved all the crew but the steward from the wrecked clipper *Sea Nymph* in 1861 by lassoing them one at a time with his riata and pulling them ashore. (The *Sea Nymph* was one of several ships that mistook Point Reyes for the Golden Gate in the fog.)

The trail to the lagoon, an old ranch road, begins at a hiker's stile and runs across open pasture through another one. In a mile you arrive at the narrow passage between the upper and lower parts of the lagoon. A bridge crosses over to the sand dune on the other side.

Now you can walk across the dunes toward the ocean. A glorious sweep of clean driftwood beach stretches for miles in either direction. Since it is impossible to reach this spot without walking at least a mile, you can be sure that the strand will be blissfully uncrowded. A low sandbar normally separates the lagoon from the ocean, but during heavy storms the waves occasionally wash over it.

The lagoon and the beach are both fascinating to birders, especially during the fall migrations. Animal fanciers may catch a glimpse of the feral Barbary goats that inhabit the hill behind the lagoon.

## Kehoe Beach

*How to get there:* The small parking lot is 2 miles north of the Abbotts Lagoon parking lot. (People often have to park on the roadside.)

*Facilities:* Toilets at parking lot.

*Regulations:* Dogs on leash permitted on beach. No swimming or wading because of the dangerous surf.

The path to the beach leads along a creek running through a swampy area.

**Beachcombing between Abbotts Lagoon and Kehoe Beach**

Soon you reach a small lagoon. Winter storms pile up driftwood logs here in wild formation. A half mile from the parking lot you arrive at the white sandy beach. Kehoe is actually the northern end of the strand that is variously called Point Reyes Beach, the Great Beach, and Ten Mile, Eleven Mile, and Twelve Mile Beach. You can walk south almost as far as the lighthouse, but to the north your passage is blocked about a mile from the entrance trail by granite cliffs jutting into the ocean.

You can also stretch yours legs by hiking on the bluffs above the beach. An obvious trail leads off from the right of the entrance trail just before you get to the beach. You can wander over cowpaths or cross-country (being careful not to go too close to the edge of the cliff). These hillsides are a mass of wildflowers in spring—baby-blue-eyes, suncups, wild hollyhock, and iris. In winter, the cliffs offer a good vantage point to watch for whales.

## McClures Beach

*How to get there:* Drive to the end of Pierce Point Road; the parking lot for the beach is just below that for Upper Pierce Ranch.

*Facilities:* Water, toilets, phone at Upper Pierce Ranch.

*Regulations:* No dogs; no swimming or wading because of the dangerous surf.

Like Kehoe Beach, McClures is reached by a half-mile-long trail from a parking lot; and as at Kehoe, the trail follows the course of a stream. Growing on the bank to your right as you walk down are buckwheat, morning glory, lizardtail, and gumweed.

The beautiful beach is less than a mile long, being blocked at either end by unclimbable granite cliffs projecting into the ocean. At low tide you can walk through a defile in the rocks at the south end to a pocket beach. Here you may see cormorants perched on Elephant Rock and the other offshore stacks. Exploring tidepool life is another popular activity at McClures Beach.

## Upper Pierce Ranch

*How to get there:* Drive to the end of Pierce Point Road.

*Facilities:* Water, restrooms, phone, self-guiding historical trail, all wheelchair-accessible; open sunrise to sunset daily. Check at the visitor centers to see when the park plans to hold a special Dairy Day here..

*Regulations:* No dogs.

The restored ranch is now officially the Upper Pierce Ranch; the Lower Pierce Ranch, now demolished, is about 3 miles north on the Pierce Point Trail. The nomenclature is somewhat confusing, because on maps the Lower

*Oystercatchers enjoy tidepooling at McClures Beach*

Ranch is above the Upper Ranch—although it is indeed lower in elevation!

The road and the ranches are named for Solomon Pierce, who in 1858 bought 2200 acres on the point for $7000 and established a model dairy ranch. By 1878 it was the largest single dairy operation in West Marin and was famed for the high quality of its butter. Originally the ranch products (mainly butter) were taken to a landing at the foot of White Gulch, on the east side of the point, and thence by schooner to San Francisco. After the North Pacific Coast Railroad reached the east side of Tomales Bay in 1875 the ranch products went across the bay to the train, then to Sausalito, and finally by ferry to San Francisco.

As Jack Mason described the ranch in *Point Reyes: The Solemn Land*, it must have been impressive indeed, virtually a self-contained village: in addition to 300 cows, it had "a blacksmith shop, model cow and horse barns, a carpenter shop where butter boxes were made, a schoolhouse, a laundry with a Chinese in charge, and a warehouse stocked with sugar, tea, syrups, flour and other provender that reminded one visitor of a country store."

After being in the Pierce family's possession for three generations, the ranch was bought by James McClure in 1929. After a few years of dairy operation, the McClure family, instead of butter, raised hogs and beef cattle. In 1973 the NPS bought the ranch and eventually decided to restore its buildings and make it an educational center for the history of Point Reyes dairies.

As you wander around the ranch on the self-guiding tour you may feel as if carried back by time machine into the 19th century. Explanatory plaques describe the uses of the various barns and sheds, the blacksmith shop, the one-room schoolhouse, and other buildings. The original ranch house is now occupied by park personnel.

## Tomales Point (Pierce Point) Trail

*How to get there:* The trailhead is west of the Upper Pierce Ranch.

*Facilities:* Water, toilets, phone at trailhead; no water anywhere along the route.

*Regulations:* No dogs.

Most of this trail is actually the old road that linked the upper and lower model dairy ranches operated by the Pierce family for three generations. A plaque at the trailhead advises hikers of the possibility of encountering a mountain lion. These animals have occasionally been sighted here, but none has ever attacked a person; rather, they usually run away. You are much more likely to see some tule elk, which are fenced in at the point. The original herd has grown from 13 in 1977 to well over 100. They wander around unpredictably; if you are really eager to see them, ask the rangers where they have been sighted recently. One day some of us walked the entire 9 miles to the end of point and back, hoping to catch a glimpse of elk, and saw none until we arrived back at the parking lot—they were on the hillside on the other side of the road!

The trip to the end of the point is about 4½ miles long. It's quite level, highly scenic, entirely open, and often windy and foggy. Bring a waterproof windbreaker, plus binoculars if you own them.

The trail runs uphill among clumps of lupine, to the west of Upper Pierce Ranch. When you come to the old road, veer left on it. It ascends gradually for a mile. You can look down over McClures Beach and an inaccessible beach to its north.

As the road continues its gentle ascent it passes granitic outcroppings on the low hills. If your imagination is running wild you can easily fancy that these are ancient Celtic tumuli, from which a Druid or one of the Little People might pop up at any moment. The eeriness of the scene is heightened when you discover a line of granitic boulders running almost straight, due north and south, on either side of the road as far as the eye can see. Don Schinske of the *Point Reyes Light* did some research on this mysterious wall of boulders, which has puzzled hikers for years. He noted (issue of March 17, 1994) that the bayward line points directly to Mt. St. Helena, 60 miles away. One theory—although so far pure conjecture—is that the wall was built by the Coast Miwok. Mt. St. Helena was important to them as a source of obsidian, which they used for arrowheads.

As you walk along, you enjoy superb and ever-changing views of Tomales Bay. Just offshore to the east is two-plus-acre Hog Island. According to historian Jack Mason's *Earthquake Bay*, "By most accounts it got its name when a barge broke loose, depositing its cargo of porkers on the beach." During the late 19th and early 20th centuries the Hulbe family lived on the island. They finally gave up because of the scarcity of water and the distance from medical care. After the Hulbes, the island passed through a series of owners. One of them built a house on the east side, the remains of which can still be seen. Somewhere along the line the island got forested with eucalyptus—obviously not its natural vegetation. The Audubon Society acquired it in 1972, and in 1996 donated it to the National Seashore. It may continue in its present state, uninhabited but a magnet to daytime visitors in kayaks, canoes, and sailboats. The little island south of Hog is officially named Duck Island, but the locals sometimes refer to it as Piglet.

White Gulch, an inlet on the shore just west of Hog Island, was the original landing for the Pierce Ranch complex. From 1904 to 1941 it was the site of the Tomales Point Gun Club. Herbert Hoover was one of its distinguished guests.

Across Tomales Bay you can see Toms Point and to its north Sand Point, with the village of Dillon Beach on the slope above it. Still farther north is Bodega Head. On the right side of Sand Point is Lawson's Landing, which consists mainly of a huge trailer park. The dunes above it are occasionally frequented by hang gliders, and one afternoon as we lunched atop a Tomales Point hillock we watched a few dozen boldly colored gliders seeking vainly for a favorable wind, only to plunge ignominiously back into the dunes.

Now the road descends gradually toward Lower Pierce Ranch, passes a pond, and peters out into a trail. About a mile beyond the ranch it arrives at a bluff just across from Bird Rock, a large offshore stack usually inhabited by cormorants. One New Year's Day a group of us hiked here hoping to see migrating whales; we drew a blank on the whales, but instead saw a huge flock of white pelicans on Bird Rock. A path leads down the steep 200-foot cliff to a small beach here; ignore it—it's too dangerous.

From Bird Rock to the end of the point is less than a mile. The trail more or less disappears in a broad patch of sand, but you can proceed cross-country to the bluff overlooking the entrance to Tomales Bay. Here you can lounge at leisure with your lunch, watching boats and looking for seals and interesting birds, to the accompaniment of the plangent, faintly melancholy clang of a bell buoy.

On the hike mentioned above, the air was so clear at the bluff that looking southeast we could see Mt. Tamalpais in the distance above Hog Island; but by the time we had retraced our steps as far as Lower Pierce Ranch fog had completely enveloped us, and by the time we reached the parking lot those of us who had not brought along waterproof windbreakers were completely soaked. This sort of rapid, unpredictable weather change is par for the course on Tomales Point, and one should come prepared.

*Heading for the tip of Tomales Point, with Bodega Head visible to the north*

# Five Brooks

*How to get there:* The trailhead is just off Highway 1, 3½ miles south of Olema. Coming north on Highway 1, Five Brooks is about 5 miles beyond the (usually unmarked) turnoff to Bolinas at the north end of Bolinas Lagoon.

*Facilities:* Water, toilets, a few picnic tables. There is no water on most of the trails around here. Five Brooks Stables offers guided trail rides (phone 663-1570).

*Regulations:* No dogs on trails; no open fires, no motor vehicles, no firearms; camping by permit only, free at Bear Valley Visitor Center.

Geologist Alan Galloway points out: "At Five Brooks, as the name implies, the drainage is very complex and is undoubtedly affected by fault movements. . .Olema Creek and Pine Gulch Creek run parallel to one another in opposite directions, separated only by about 1500 feet . . . ." Some of the trails from Five Brooks lead along these capricious creeks; other ascend Inverness Ridge and run along it.

This southern part of the park is full of old trails that are unmaintained, unsigned, and unmapped. The main hazards in venturing on them are poison oak and ticks.

## Rift Zone Trail

One of the most attractive trails out of Five Brooks is the 4½-mile Rift Zone Trail running north to Bear Valley. This trail is described on pp. 47–48. To get on it from the Five Brooks end, head north from the parking lot past a pond fringed with willows, and in less than 100 yards bear right on a path signed BEAR VALLEY TRAIL THROUGH VEDANTA RETREAT.

## Trails to Firtop and beyond

Most of the trails in the Five Brooks area are reached by circling counterclockwise around the mill pond near the parking lot. (On one occasion we saw a large turtle sunning himself on a rock in this pond.) The pond dates back to the 1950s, when a lumber company floated logs across it to their sawmill. Marin County had recently passed a tax on standing timber, so many owners either started logging or sold their timber rights. The Sweet Company of Oregon bought rights to thousands of acres on Inverness Ridge and busily set about logging the Douglas firs. When the President authorized the park in 1962 logging ceased, and now the visitor to Five Brooks hears only the chirp of birds and the occasional neigh of horses instead of the whining of chainsaws. Hikers along the trails will see that young Douglas firs are replacing the original forest.

Partway around the pond, signs point the way to Olema Valley on the left and the Stewart Trail on the right. To get to Firtop take the Stewart Trail. This is an old ranch road, improved by the Army during World War II, that climbs gradually up

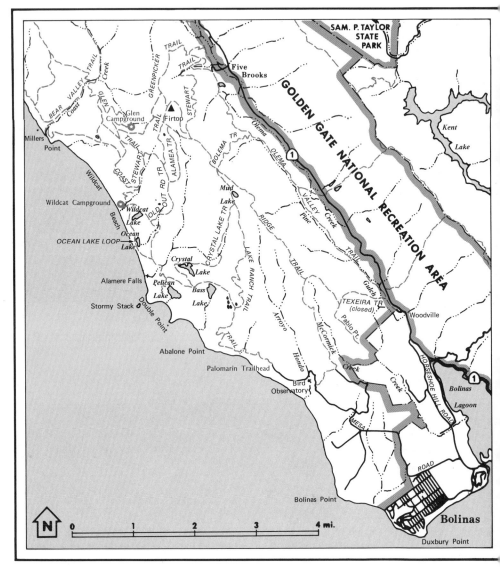

**TRAILS FROM FIVE BROOKS AND PALOMARIN**
# MAP 7

LEGEND: Roads
Trail
Park Bdy.
⊙ Campground

through ferny forest, crossing one of the five brooks on its way. After about a mile you reach a junction with the Greenpicker Trail, and now you can choose which way to proceed to Firtop.

The Stewart Trail is somewhat more gradual. After a couple of miles it emerges on the Ridge Trail. From here you turn right to reach Firtop in less than a mile. The Greenpicker Trail is

*Turtles sometimes sunbathe on a log in a pond at the Five Brooks trailhead*

somewhat shorter, steeper and narrower—more of a true trail. Part of it climbs along the edge of the Vedanta Society's retreat. It levels off in a corridor of young Douglas firs to reach Firtop.

Firtop (1324') is a broad, level meadow surrounded by fir trees. It's a pleasant place for lunch, and if you have enough to eat, drink, and read you might want to spend the afternoon here. Firtop is also a major trail junction, offering several options:

You can return to Five Brooks via whichever trail you did not take coming up.

You can take the gently rolling Ridge Trail south for a mile and a half to a three-way junction in a parklike forest, and turn left on the Bolema Trail. It runs steeply down the ridge and turns left on the Olema Valley Trail to return to Five Brooks. (This would constitute a loop of about 7 miles. A hiker who took this loop during a wet spring commented that it was unpleasantly full of mud and horse manure. Some of this unpleasantness might be avoided by going one way on the steeper, narrower Greenpicker Trail.)

If you have a camping permit from the Bear Valley Visitor Center you can take the Greenpicker Trail and then the Glen Trail to Glen Camp. Or (again with a camping permit) you can take the Stewart Trail to the Coast Trail and Wildcat Camp—a highly scenic route overlooking the sea.

If you're game for a variegated and scenic hike of over 10 miles, arrange a car shuttle and leave one car at Palomarin trailhead. From Firtop take the Alamea and Old Out trails, or the Ridge and Lake Ranch trails, to the Coast Trail and on to Palomarin. Of course you can reverse these routes by leaving one car at Five Brooks.

## Olema Valley Trail

*How to get there:* This trail might be considered a continuation of the Rift Zone Trail. It runs for 5½ fairly level miles along the San Andreas fault zone through a delightful mixture of forest and farmland. Unless you want to retrace your steps, the easiest way to do this hike is by car shuttle. Take both cars to the southern end of the trail, 4½ miles south of the Five Brooks turnoff (if driving north, a long half mile north of Horseshoe Hill Road). A sign on the west side of Highway 1 announces the Olema Valley Trail and just across the highway another sign announces the McCurdy Trail going up Bolinas Ridge in GGNRA land. The road here is wide enough for a few cars to park. Leave one car here and take the other car to Five Brooks.

(Note that the southern part of the trail includes two creek fordings that might present problems during the rainy season. On my last visit a small, discreet sign at the southern trailhead advised HAZARDOUS TRAIL; we did not notice this sign until we had finished hiking from Five Brooks and got our shoes somewhat wet crossing the springtime creek.)

*Facilities:* Water, toilets, picnic tables at Five Brooks; none along the trail.

From Five Brooks trailhead turn left at the fountain—that is, the circular horse fountain commemorating "Sonny" Zappetini, a San Rafael ironworker and dedicated horseman. Walk clockwise around the mill pond, where you may also see frogs and turtles, and go left on the signed Olema Valley Trail. It begins as a broad, level, leafy path, at times under a virtual tunnel of alder, bay, and hazel trees.

After crossing a creek on a bridge the trail climbs for a half mile—the only fairly steep part of this walk. A little over a mile from the trailhead you reach a signed junction with the Bolema Trail, which heads uphill to join the Ridge Trail while the Olema Valley Trail goes downhill to the left. Now the broad path undulates over old fields dotted with Douglas firs and coyote brush. You can look over to Bolinas Ridge on the east, and Highway 1 is occasionally visible and audible. Just before you reach a cypress windbreak (site of an 1850s ranch established by Spaniard Pablo Figueras), a hiker's symbol advises you to bear right. Soon a sign indicates the junction with the Randall spur trail leading to Highway 1. The path turns into a true trail, rather than a broad wagon track, as it traverses a pleasant forest of oaks and bays alternating with grassy glades.

During some of this journey you have been walking between the two streams that geologist Alan Galloway cites as examples of the fault zone's complex drainage system: "In this area, Olema Creek and Pine Gulch Creek run parallel to one another in opposite directions, separated only by about 1500 feet, with Olema Creek flowing into Tomales Bay to the north and Pine Gulch Creek into Bolinas Lagoon to the south." And a look at the USGS maps will reveal that many of the streams make odd right-angle bends when they reach the fault zone. By this point on the trail you can hear Pine Gulch Creek bubbling merrily on your right, oblivious to its geologic peculiarity, and soon you ford it and cross a field behind a handsome farmhouse. The trail passes a junction with

*Young second-growth firs line the Glen Camp Trail west of Firtop*

the Teixeira Trail—now officially closed. The Olema Valley Trail now fords the creek again and skirts a large marsh. It runs near the edge of the highway, then crosses another field to reach the Dogtown trailhead.

This hamlet appears on the topo as Woodville, but on more recent maps as Dogtown. In the 1850s and '60s this was a rip-roaring lumbering town. The late historian Jack Mason claimed that the original name was Dogtown but that in 1868 the citizens, hoping to attract marriageable women, officially changed it to the more genteel Woodville. In the 1970s the inhabitants decided to rechristen it with the more dramatic Dogtown.

**Trail riders take a break at Wildcat Camp**

# Palomarin

*How to get there:*

- *Northbound:* From Stinson Beach proceed north on Highway 1 for 4½ miles and at the Bolinas turnoff (usually unsigned) go left for 1¾ miles to Mesa Road, on your right, before reaching Bolinas proper. Follow Mesa to its end, 4½ miles north.
- *Southbound:* From Olema go south on Highway 1 for 9 miles to the Bolinas turnoff, turn right, and proceed as above.

Along the way you pass several communications towers that look like artifacts from Alpha Centauri; the Niman-Schell Ranch, which produces quality beef for the Bay Area's best restaurants; and a windowless, half-sunken Coast Guard radio station with a faintly sinister aspect.

The Palomarin Ranch was originally O. L. Shafter's South End Ranch. In 1950 it was purchased by the Church of the Golden Rule, which developed a sizable self-contained community here, including houses, barns, schools, and a nursery business. The NPS bought the ranch in 1963 and in '64 destroyed most of the buildings except for one of the schools, which now houses the Point Reyes Bird Observatory.

## Point Reyes Bird Observatory

Phone: 868-1221
Fax: 868-1946

*Facilities:* Open daily, free, 7 A.M.–5 P.M.; bird banding 7 A.M.–1 P.M.; water, restrooms, phone, nature trail.

Point Reyes Bird Observatory is a nonprofit membership-supported organization devoted to the study and conservation of wildlife—particularly seabirds, landbirds, and marine mammals. One of its most valuable functions is to act as guardian for the Farallon Islands 20 miles offshore. The Farallones support the largest seabird colony in the continental United States, as well as sizable populations of seals and sea lions. Before the PRBO took them under its wing, so to speak, these birds and animals were being hunted and harassed by humans.

Palomarin Beach, ½ mile west of the observatory, is one of the few places in the Seashore you can take your dog, on leash (but you can't camp out or park overnight). To reach the narrow beach you must walk about a mile down a graveled road. (Surfers like it, too.)

## Coast Trail to Wildcat Camp

The main Palomarin parking lot is 0.8 mile beyond the bird observatory.

*Facilities:* Toilets ⅛ mile from the trailhead. No water on trail. Wildcat Camp has water, toilets, picnic tables, grills, and hitchrails.

*Regulations:* The Palomarin area is part of the Phillip Burton Wilderness. Hence: no dogs; no bikes; no open fires; no motor vehicles; no firearms; camping by permit only, free at Bear Valley Visitor Center. Wildcat Camp is generally reserved for groups, but individuals and families may camp here in sites that groups have not reserved.

Wildcat Camp is a possible overnight backpack stop and an excellent goal for an all-day hike. The trail to it passes four freshwater lakes, and a fifth is reachable by an easy side trip. These lakes testify to the area's geologic instability, which results from its proximity to the San Andreas Fault: They were formed by earth slippages that blocked the natural drainage. (In fact, the whole Palomarin area might be considered one huge landslide.)

Wildcat Camp, like Coast, is open and treeless; its charm is its situation a few hundred feet from a splendid, uncrowded beach. (Any beach, however magnificent, that requires 5 miles or more of hiking to reach is going to be uncrowded most of the time.)

From the parking lot, full of colorful weeds, go up some steps and head for the eucalyptus grove. The toilets are on the far side of the grove. The Coast Trail, an old farm road, runs along the headlands a couple of hundred feet above the ocean. For the next 2 miles you will be walking mainly through coastal scrub— e.g., coyote brush, California sagebrush, and poison oak. There is a somewhat melancholy cast to this country, especially on a cloudy day. However, if you take the hike in spring or summer, any tendency toward gloom may be dispelled by the profusion of flowers. Along the headlands are red and yellow paintbrush, common and dwarf brodiaea, morning glory, wild cucumber, and assorted members of the sunflower family. As the season progresses, you can find clarkia, coast buckwheat, pearly everlasting, and masses of lizardtail.

After ½ mile the trail goes briefly into a little gully containing a stream. It returns to the cliffs; then a mile from the trailhead it leaves the ocean and crosses another stream graced by watercress, yellow monkey flower, and brass buttons. Now you ascend gradually along the north side of a canyon, pass through a defile among Ithuriel's spear, tidytips, and yarrow, and descend past the LAKE RANCH TRAIL (sign) on the right.

The Lake Ranch was part of O. L. Shafter's holdings. In 1940 his heirs sold it to socialite polo player William Tevis. He had a cattle ranch and timber rights on Inverness Ridge, which he sold to the Sweet Lumber Company of Oregon. They logged the Douglas firs until 1963, when the NPS condemned these timber rights. The NPS purchased the ranch in 1971 and destroyed all its buildings, including a handsome old ranch house. Now the site of the house is marked by a number of small ponds to the left of the trail that attract kildeer, swallows, and flocks of red-winged blackbirds.

Now the Coast Trail levels off, then descends gradually through alders and willows, and soon passes sheltered Bass Lake. You are not likely to find bass here nowadays, but you might find trout—and in warm weather a few skinny-dippers. A century ago you might have seen hunters and anglers. J. Smeaton Chase, in his classic *California Coast Trails: A Horseback Ride From Mexico to Oregon* (1913) describes the Lake Ranch in 1911:

**Meadow in the making at Crystal Lake**

> The country here was very interesting in appearance. A group of small fresh-water lakes lies near the shore, which rises to a picturesque moorland backed by irregular hills. Seaward, the Farallones showed like icebergs on the sky-line, and the long arm of Point Reyes marked the outline of Drakes Bay . . . . This is a magnificent game country, and the fact has not been overlooked by the sporting clubs, whose notices hailed me on all sides with threats of Severe Penalties and Utmost Rigors.

Indeed, there was a hunting lodge on the shore of Bass Lake for many years.

A quarter mile beyond Bass Lake a side trail to Crystal Lake branches off to the right. This trail is at present rather overgrown and the lake is not really crystalline. The next lake is triangular Pelican, below you to the left. As the trail leaves the lake, you can see on a clear day the whole Point Reyes peninsula spread out before you, with the stacks off Miller Point in the middle distance.

From Pelican Lake the trail descends gently, following signs with a hiker's symbol. Two side roads go off to the left to overlook Double Point and Stormy Stack—worth a side trip for the superb ocean view and a chance of seeing seals. The main Coast Trail crosses Alamere Creek. You soon come to a junction where the Ocean Lake Loop Trail splits off left from the Coast Trail. Although the Ocean Lake Loop Trail is slightly longer (both are just a bit over a mile) and has more up-and-down than the Coast Trail, it is definitely more scenic, offering views over Ocean and Wildcat lakes and the rugged coastline. Shortly after the two trails converge you descend to Wildcat Camp.

You can take a side trip by walking south on the beach to Double Point, which as you approach from this angle has a surprising resemblance to the Rock of Gibraltar. You are also approaching Alamere Falls, one of the prime jewels of the National Seashore.

## Lake Ranch and Ridge trails

*How to get there:* Begin at the Palomarin trailhead, as in the preceding hike.

*Facilities:* Toilets near trailhead; otherwise, none. Carry plenty of water; on a warm day carry twice as much as you think you'll need.

Here is a scenic 11-mile all-day loop that covers a lot of diverse terrain. If you can arrange a two-car shuttle, you can make it a one-way 7½-mile hike by leaving one car at Five Brooks trailhead and finishing on the Bolema and Olema Valley trails rather than the Ridge Trail.

For the first 2.2 miles, follow the Coast Trail, as in the previous hike. Turn right on the Lake Ranch Trail—which, like so many in the National Seashore, is an old farm road—and begin a steady ascent through coastal scrub plus poppies, lupine, and cow parsnip. As you climb, you get ever-widening views of the peninsula.

The trail levels off in a shrubby area frequented by giant jackrabbits. After two miles the Lake Ranch Trail enters a cool, shady Douglas-fir forest. Soon you pass Mud Lake, a tarn full of tule and azolla, or water fern. As one of the more bizarre effects of the 1906 quake, this lake was almost completely drained. Harold Gilliam notes, "The only clue as to what happened was that a spring on the east side of the ridge three quarters of a mile away suddenly increased greatly in volume. Since the quake, the lake has been restored by natural processes." The lake attracts lots of birds—e.g., warblers, red-winged blackbirds, and Oregon juncos.

Shortly after passing Mud Lake you come to a four-way trail junction (sign) at a rustic old gate in an almost parklike forest. This is an idyllic lunch spot. If you left one car at Five Brooks, you can reach it by taking the Bolema Trail, which runs northeast from this junction for 2½ miles down to that trailhead. Otherwise, turn southeast on the Ridge Trail, which undulates gently along the crest of the ridge. The area east of the trail was obviously logged before the NPS took it over. After a mile or so, the fir forest becomes dense again, and beneath the trees grow lots of sword ferns and huckleberries; in late summer you might harvest enough for a pie. After 2½ miles on the Ridge Trail you come to a sign indicating TEIXEIRA TRAIL, UNMAINTAINED, DANGEROUS CONDITONS.

The Ridge Trail now begins to descend, and emerges from the forest. Soon you can see the ocean on the right and the exposed ridge of Pablo Point on the other side of a very deep gorge on the left, then toylike Stinson Beach far below and eventually the City gleaming in the distance—always assuming, of course, that the fog hasn't come in. The last mile of descent, fairly steep, brings you out on the road near the bird observatory. Turn right here and walk the mile back to the trailhead.

# Tomales Bay—the East Shore

*Note:* Because many of the establishments described below keep irregular hours and some are open only on weekends, it is wise to phone ahead of your visit.

Between 1972—when the enabling legislation for the GGNRA was passed—and 1980, the late, visionary Representative Phil Burton guided five "authorized" boundary expansions through Congress. That they were "authorized" did not necessarily mean that all could immediately be acquired by the NPS or be open to public access. The largest part—the section of Olema Valley and Bolinas Ridge east of Highway 1—has been open to the public for years and is administered by the National Seashore. Subsequently the NPS has acquired more parcels of land, some in the "Lagunitas Loop" (not yet open to the public) and a few smaller ones on the eastern shore of Tomales Bay.

In 1993 long-time Marin County Supervisor Gary Giacomini proposed an optimistic plan to preserve most of the eastern shore of the bay from development: the federal government and the Marin Agricultural Land Trust (MALT – see p. 21) would combine to purchase development rights to the land as long as it remained in agricultural use. This plan would cost only an estimated one third of what it would cost to buy the land outright. Senator Barbara Boxer and Representative Lynn Woolsey introduced bills to this effect in the 103rd Congress, but before they could be acted on, the election of November 1994 resulted in a much less park-friendly legislative body. If you want to see the east shore of Tomales Bay before it acquires possible casinos, marinas, golf courses, and giant mansions, better start driving north up Highway 1 from Point Reyes Station soon!

## Tomales Bay Trail

*How to get there:* Drive north on Highway 1 for about 1¾ miles from Point Reyes Station and look for the trailhead sign on the left.

*Facilities:* Free parking.

*Regulations:* Wildlife Area: no pets, horses, camping, guns, or bicycles.

This easy and scenic 1.3-mile walk is on part of what was once the Martinelli Ranch. In 1978 Congress approved purchase of the 256-acre ranch for the GGNRA but—as so often has happened—neglected to appropriate the funds to buy it, leaving the Martinellis in limbo. A San Francisco development company took an interest in the land and proposed to construct on it 70 homes, a hotel, a restaurant, a golf course, and a polo field (!). Finally, in 1986, goaded by then-Congresswoman Barbara Boxer, Congress agreed to appropriate the funds for the GGNRA to buy it.

The trail ascends past a large rock formation, then descends to pass two ponds much favored by ducks, red-winged blackbirds, and other avian fauna. Between the two ponds the trail passes through willow, coyote brush, and *lots* of poison oak. After the second pond the trail ascends gently and curves right to arrive at the top of a hillock.

From here there is a superb view all up and down Tomales Bay, which lies atop the San Andreas Fault. You are standing on the North American Plate and looking over to the Pacific Plate, the most prominent feature in view being forested Inverness Ridge. The sight of the October 1995 Vision Fire from here was eerie and dread-inspiring.

To the east is Black (a.k.a. Elephant) Mountain, to the southeast Barnabe Peak and Mt. Tam. On the levees below you to the north are the old rights of way for the narrow-gauge North Pacific Coast Railroad, which reached here from Sausalito in 1875 and continued north to Tomales. Eventually the railroad extended to Cazadero, in the (then) prime redwood forests of Sonoma County. It continued running under various ownerships until the last train left Point Reyes Station in 1933.

After returning to the parking lot, you continue north on Highway 1. Just north of the Martinelli Ranch was the once-flourishing oystering community of Bivalve, which still remains on some maps. During the early 20th century the Pacific Oyster Company sent daily shipments to San Francisco on the railroad.

## Millerton Point and Alan Sieroty Beach

*How to get there:* Go north on Highway 1 for 4¾ miles from Point Reyes Station and look for the entrance on the left, marked by a state-park sign.

*Facilities:* Picnic tables, toilets, free parking.

*Regulations:* This park is actually an adjunct to Tomales Bay State Park across the bay; the usual state-park rules apply, including no dogs on beaches or trails.

The beach is named for retired state senator Alan Sieroty, a dedicated conservationist. The point itself is named for a prominent early rancher, James Miller. From the parking lot and picnic area one trail leads left over a footbridge to the beach; another (an old farm road) leads up a knoll from which you can view Inverness across the bay and the various beaches of Tomales Bay State Park proper.

Perhaps the most unusual feature of this park is the osprey nest on a platform that PG&E specially constructed when ospreys kept nesting on their power poles and at one time shorted out power to Inverness for a couple of hours. PG&E very painstakingly erected a suitable nesting site on a pole about 100 feet from the original nest and encouraged the ospreys to move there. On my last visit an osprey pair were happily feeding their young atop the new pole. Of course birds are notoriously flighty, so you can't be absolutely sure they will be there when you visit. But even if they aren't, the park offers a pleasant walk.

Just beyond Millerton Point is the Tomales Bay Oyster Company, established in 1923 and still selling oysters wholesale to restaurants and retail to visitors (663-1242).

## Marconi Conference Center

*How to get there:* Go north on Highway 1 for another 2½ miles and look for the entrance on the right.

Marconi has a most unusual history. In 1913 Guglielmo Marconi, inventor of the "wireless telegraph" (radio), picked this hillside on which to build his Pacific

Coast receiving station for messages from Hawaii, Asia, and ships at sea. In 1914 he constructed an impressive Mediterranean-style building for his staff and guests. It was popularly known as "the hotel," although apparently it was never open to the general public. In 1920 the Radio Corporation of America bought the property and soon sold all but 62 acres of it to a local rancher. Subsequently RCA moved its facilities to G Ranch on the Point Reyes peninsula, where you can see them (now under the sign of MCI) as you drive along Sir Francis Drake Highway.

The Marconi property then passed through a series of owners, including a retired Portuguese consul, until 1964 when it was purchased by the Synanon Foundation. Synanon had begun as a rehabilitation group for substance abusers. After it moved to Marconi and bought two nearby ranches, stories began to circulate about its cultlike aspects, including child abuse and violence against perceived opponents. One of their more notorious acts was to plant a live rattlesnake in the mailbox of an attorney they were feuding with; he was bitten but survived. The *Point Reyes Light* diligently investigated Synanon's activities and in 1979 received the Pulitzer Prize for its exposé. Beleaguered by lawsuits and declining finances, Synanon sold all its Marin properties in 1981 to the Buck Fund, which after much complicated negotiation turned it over to the state-park system for use as a conference center.

It is indeed a handsome place in which to hold a conference, and the rates seem very reasonable. Nonconferees may visit the grounds and hike along scenic trails overlooking Tomales Bay and the Marin hills.

Marconi Conference Center
Box 789, Marshall, CA 94940
Phone: 663-9020
Fax: 663-1731

## Beyond Marconi Conference Center. . . .

Just 0.4 mile north on Highway 1 from the conference center on the bay side of the road is the venerable and popular Tony's Seafood Restaurant (663-1107). Just beyond it are the Marshall Boat Works, Tamal Saka kayak rentals (663-1743), and a small general store (663-1339). (Tamal Saka gets its name from the Coast Miwok for bay, Tamal, and tule reed boats, Saka.)

Next you arrive at what was once the center of the town of Marshall (called Marshalls on some old maps). It was founded in the 1850s by five brothers from Ireland, and by the time the railroad arrived in 1875 was already a flourishing village. The center of activity for much of the town's existence was the hotel, originally built in 1870 and rebuilt after a fire in 1896; unfortunately it burned down again in 1971. The adjoining Marshall Tavern still stands, but barely.

Just beyond the old tavern building is the Hog Island Oyster Company (663-9218) and Marshall Arts, a small community center that sometimes has weekend evening entertainment (663-1318).

Continuing north on Highway 1, 0.6 mile past the Marshall-Petaluma Road on the right is the Cypress Grove Preserve (CGP) on the left. The beautiful Victorian buildings—barely visible from the highway—and surrounding land were deeded to Audubon Canyon Ranch by Clifford Conly. The preserve is managed from the ranch headquarters near Bolinas Bay, and at present it is not generally open to the public. However, it is sometimes possible to visit it *by appointment only* (663-8203).

About 3½ miles farther along is Nick's Cove, which contains another venerable and popular seafood restaurant (663-1033). Just above Nick's is Miller County Park (moderate fee), with boat-launching facilities, a fishing pier, picnic tables, and toilets.

Shortly before the highway turns inland it passes the abandoned buildings of Hamlet on the left. It was so named not for the Danish prince or because it was such a tiny town but because rancher John Hamlet owned property here in the 1870s; it contained a train depot and a post office. For many years during the 20th century it was the site of Jensen's Oyster Beds. In 1987 the GGNRA bought the property, and may in future open it to the public.

If you continue inland on Highway 1 you will soon reach the picturesque village of Tomales—so picturesque, in fact, that the Smithsonian Institution has called it "a case study of California regional architecture." You may want to stroll around and enjoy the old churches and the Victorian houses. Tomales contains a couple of restaurants and some lodging facilities.

### Recommended reading

Mason, Jack, *Earthquake Bay*, 2nd ed. Inverness: North Shore Books, 1980.

(I owe many thanks to David and Ellen Elliott, homeowners in Marshall, for their companionship and assistance in describing the east shore of Tomales Bay; and as always to the ever-helpful National Seashore Historian Dewey Livingston.)

# Index